THE LAST
ROMAN

THE LAST ROMAN

ROMULUS AUGUSTULUS AND THE DECLINE OF THE WEST

ADRIAN MURDOCH

SUTTON PUBLISHING

First published in the United Kingdom in 2006 by
Sutton Publishing Limited · Phoenix Mill
Thrupp · Stroud · Gloucestershire · GL5 2BU

British Library Cataloguing in Publication Data
A catalogue record for this book is available from the British Library.

ISBN 0-7509-4474-9

Typeset in 11/15pt Sabon.
Typesetting and origination by
Sutton Publishing Limited.
Printed and bound in England by
J.H. Haynes & Co. Ltd, Sparkford.

For Susy

'As father of my country I will probably be Rome's last emperor. For that reason alone, I occupy a rather forlorn position in world history. No matter what happens I shall end up with a bad reputation.'

Friedrich Dürrenmatt, *Romulus the Great*

'Romulus Augustulus!' the polymath had said. 'What a name! Poor chap, he was very good-looking, it seems, and only sixteen.'

Patrick Leigh Fermor, *A Time of Gifts*

Contents

INTRODUCTION

It's the End of the World as We Know It

In the spring of AD 477, the sea lanes across the Mediterranean opened again after the winter storms. Making one of the first voyages of the year, a ship docked at the harbour near the Great Palace in Constantinople. On board were senators from Rome with a letter for Emperor Zeno, head of the Eastern Roman empire.

New Rome, as Constantinople or Byzantium was dubbed, had been the capital of the empire for the past 147 years. Constantine's city had been formally dedicated in the summer of AD 330 at the time of his silver jubilee. No longer was it a new town with the whiff of paint, the strange scent of drying plaster, the dust of marble being shaped, the noise of carpenters, masons and engineers. It was the seat of government, the emperor and his court. The army chiefs of staff were based there, as were the law courts.

The city had been adorned with all the trappings of the power and the glory. Wide-open forums, streets protected with colonnades, squares decorated with columns and statues recalling battles won and generals honoured. There were massive and sprawling public buildings, palaces, important monasteries as well as the structures necessary to keep a growing urban population entertained. Byzantium boasted 4,388 individual homes to Rome's 1,800 – roughly two and a half times more. There were baths and theatres as well as the most famous building of all, the hippodrome in the centre of town, right in front of the Great Palace.

1

The diplomats did not approach Constantinople via the Golden Gate, the monumental ceremonial entrance to the city made of polished marble. They arrived, as everyone should, by sea, coming up the south-facing Marmara coast – increasingly the right address in this period, especially if you wanted protection from the winds that howled down from the north for most of the winter.

As they sailed closer to shore, they saw why Byzantium was growing fat, rich on the profits from the sea trade that had to pass through the Bosphorus Straits. Not only was it the land bridge between East and West, it was the sea link between north and south. The senators passed two huge artificial harbours named after previous emperors, Theodosius I and Julian the Apostate, filled with ships from the East with their cargoes of grain – centuries away from the oil tankers that now ply their trade up and down the straits.

From on board they heard the shouts and noises of workmen in the massive granaries, the Horrea Alexandrina and the state-controlled Horreum Theodosianum that stretched between the two harbours and that handled the shipments of Egyptian wheat coming up from the south to feed the city.

Only then could they see the capital of the empire in its full imposing glory. It is difficult to imagine the cultural and open-mouthed awe that a visit to the world's most important city inspired, especially for visitors from the increasingly unpolished West. By the reign of the Emperor Justinian in the sixth century, Constantinople would boast a population of 500,000, causing one historian to grumble about the metropolis's 'unnecessarily large population'. Several years earlier, a barbarian, up to then a committed opponent of the empire, was invited to visit and became a stunned convert. 'I see now what my unbelieving ears have often heard about,' he said. Shocked by the sights he added: 'The emperor really is a god on earth and whoever lifts a hand against him is guilty of suicide.' This was the effect that the city desired, that it expected.

Far to their left as they approached the harbour, the senators would have been aware of the walls that protected Byzantium, 6.5 kilometres long and running from the Golden Horn to the Sea of Marmara. Some 12 metres high and 5 metres thick they were protected by almost a hundred towers. The walls had seen off various barbarians, just as they were to see off Bulgar and Arab hordes in years to come. Indeed, they were not to suffer any breach until the mid-fifteenth century. Built fifty-five years before this visit by Theodosius II, they are visible to this day, the sole mute reminder of that emperor's reign. The diplomats must have been conscious that this was a security sadly lacking in the West.

As they came into port, they could see the church of St Sophia in the distance. This was not the structure that we know today, commissioned by the Emperor Justinian and designed by Isidore of Miletus, the glorious building with a thousand lamps and the famous dome that embraces the church. That was another sixty years away. What caught their attention was the second church on that spot to bear the name. The original had been burned down by protesters three generations previously, angry at the imperial banishment of the popular if provocative cleric John Chrysostom. This one was a pentagonal basilica with a columned entrance that housed the bones of Joseph, famous for his coat of many colours, and Zachariah, father of John the Baptist. The building was to survive another fifty-five years until it became the victim yet again of protesters in the great riots of 532.

When they disembarked they went directly into the Great Palace. The sprawling, multi-storeyed palace now lies underneath the modern Sultanahmet district. The basic layout of the building, or rather the buildings the diplomats would have seen was first determined by Emperor Constantine, who modelled it on the Flavian Palace in Rome. It soon housed a collection of state buildings with courtyards, colonnaded porticos, throne rooms and audience chambers, religious structures, gardens, libraries, assembly buildings, reception rooms and even thermal baths, all of which was loosely organised in a terraced park. Most of our information about the palace's layout comes from the tenth century and a book of ceremonies detailing paths that had to be taken through the palace for different occasions. But it is frustratingly vague and despite the quantity of academic ink that has been spilt since, no consensus has been reached on what exactly the palace looked like.

In one of the palace's many reception rooms, possibly even the most important of all, the Magnaura, the envoys would have walked up the flight of steps, through the large forecourt surrounded by porticos to the basilical audience chamber to present their credentials. Although we do not know their names, we do know about their mission. They had been sent by the new king of Italy, Odovacer, to placate the East. Odovacer was an upstart, a rebel and a barbarian. He was also the new ruler of Rome.

Odovacer had instructed the embassy to take the message that there was no longer any need for an empire divided between Byzantium and Ravenna, the north Italian city that had replaced Rome as the de facto capital in AD 402. One shared emperor, based in Byzantium, was enough. The new ruler of Italy had gone to the boy emperor he had displaced and exiled to Misenum on the bay of Capri and ordered him to sign the letter. The teenage Romulus Augustulus, the last Western Roman emperor, had been encouraged to write that he had picked Odovacer, a man of 'military and political experience', to safeguard the affairs of Italy. If it pleased the emperor, then Odovacer could be given the title of patrician, commander-in-chief and imperial deputy, and be entrusted with the government of Rome. It was a clever way for Odovacer to secure both imperial approval and to keep Constantinople at a distance. The tortured feelings of the hapless youth he had coerced would have been of little concern.

To show his faith, Odovacer's envoys handed over all the imperial regalia that had been worn by the emperor in the West: his gold and gem-encrusted belt, the sacred white robe with precious border and his purple and gold cloak. This was a deferential and significant step. Without television or mass media, a man was defined and identified by the way that he looked. As a symbol of government, hierarchy and official status, even the imperial cloak clasp – a gold brooch with three pendants – had a special importance and achieved such a prominence that it was highlighted on the coinage of emperors in the fifth and six centuries. The regalia itself has not survived, but it can be best seen in a silver plate called the Missorium of Theodosius in the Real Academia de la Historia in Madrid. The image may date to the previous century, but it clearly depicts what the Western Roman emperor might have worn on official occasions. Odovacer was handing Emperor Zeno the heart of the West.

Negotiations did not proceed as smoothly as Odovacer might have hoped. If Roman rule in the West had ended with a whimper rather than a bang the previous year, its aftermath was a series of petty diplomatic negotiations that must have bored the emperor. Zeno, in his late 40s or early 50s, had much greater problems closer to home than playing referee to a spat on the other side of the world. He had just regained power after a twenty-month exile and was hated by pretty much everyone, including most of his own family. Throughout his seventeen-year reign he was, as one historian has put it, permanently threatened by 'civil riots, military conspiracies, rebellions, invasions, usurpations and civil war'.

Embarrassingly for them, during the days that Odovacer's ambassadors were petitioning the emperor, another set of diplomatic representatives appeared. These had sailed from Salona, which was then home to Julius Nepos. Probably in his late 40s at this time, the man who had himself fallen from the peak of imperial power in a military coup and been exiled from Italy, had been living quietly as a private citizen for the past eighteen months in what is now the Croatian coastal town of Split. These new envoys were asking Zeno for money and for troops to claim back the throne. In short, they were asking for approval to invade Italy.

The emperor had to make a decision. Julius Nepos was family, but having himself only recently recovered the throne after a coup, the support he had to offer to problems outside the walled confines of Constantinople could only be moral. Under the circumstances, the solution Zeno came up with was elegant – at least from his point of view. He granted Odovacer's wish and publicly recognised him as patrician, but told him, in turn, to recognise Julius Nepos as emperor of the West. It was a meaningless gesture. Noticeably lacking were any troops or money for either side, and Nepos had to remain in Split.

So it was that the last Roman to sit on the throne of Augustus, Trajan and Constantine found his title and his regalia traded almost carelessly as a pawn in a game of diplomacy.[1]

*   *   *

Romulus Augustulus is one of the most important figures in European history. The end of his reign marked, wrote Britain's greatest historian Edward Gibbon, 'the extinction of the Roman empire in the West'. No Roman ever ruled the West again after he was deposed in 476, and Romulus is the human symbol, the name that is used for the fall of the Roman Empire. Once he had been forced to abdicate, Europe was free to welcome the Middle Ages. Romulus has been eulogised, he has been mocked, he has been dismissed, but it is impossible to read his story without a sense of loss.

It is not known when he was born; it is not known when he died; it is not even known where he was buried. No speeches, pronouncements or epigrams have survived.

There is no hint of his likes or dislikes; there is no hint of sexuality, conventional or otherwise, to add a frisson of historical excitement; there is not even any particularly gory violence. One nineteenth-century historian rightly calls the history of Byzantium a 'monotonous story of the intrigues of priests, eunuchs and women; of poisonings, of conspiracies, of uniform ingratitude, of perpetual fratricide'.[2] The final sigh in the West could offer nothing so thrilling.

We do not really know what he looked like. All we can say with certainty is that he was young, a lad under the age of 14. Indeed the sole definite descriptive statement that has survived is that he was good-looking.[3]

Only one image of him remains: the stylised portrait of a boy on a coin. But even this is of little use. At the start of the fourth century, the imperial heads on coins began to celebrate the position, not the person, they depicted, the emperor rather than an emperor. Gone are the vigorous, naturalistic representations of the Julio-Claudian or Flavian emperors. Instead, Roman mints stamped out pretty much interchangeable figures that face you with little hint of characterised likenesses. You would stare in vain though the glass of a coin cabinet for any hint of the man behind the stamp.

In fact, if all contemporary writings – a phrase used here most generously as many of the writings date to the sixth century – that mention him by name were gathered together, they would fill, at most, a couple of pages.

Much of the history of the period has come down to us from the pens of chroniclers, brief telegraphic notes, a little like newspaper headlines, of what happened in a given year. For his commentary of the year 476, Count Marcellinus, both a chronicler and a senior bureaucrat in the court of the Emperor Justinian, notes what has become Romulus' best-known epitaph. He was writing just over fifty years after the events but

Marcellinus is the first writer to make the connection between Romulus and the end of the empire explicit:

> With this Augustulus perished the western empire of the Roman people, which the first Augustus, Octavian, began to rule in the seven hundred and ninth year from the foundation of the city. This occurred in the five hundred and twenty-second year of the kingdom of the departed emperor, with Gothic kings thereafter holding Rome.[4]

A sadness emerges in a brief and impersonal snippet like this. The diminutive and affectionate if slightly dismissive *-ulus* at the end of his name, which was added by later chroniclers, captures both his age and his lack of importance. But as with a marriage breaking up, the West had not accepted what Byzantium knew: that this marked the end of the relationship. It still thought that another emperor might appear. Appearances were kept up, the pretence that it was a trial separation for the sake of the provinces; but ultimately it was doomed.

It is valid to ask whether one should attempt to write something that purports to be a biography about a character of whom we know so little. The answer has to be yes for three reasons. The first is that the drawn-out collapse of the Western empire makes it easy to forget the human aspect. All too often, historians get lost in the sweep of events, the broad brush strokes of barbarian settlements, military retrenchment and economic turmoil. Focusing on Romulus and his family gives a different and more personal perspective to the fall of the Roman Empire.

The second reason is a growing interest – popular rather than just scholarly – in this period of late antiquity. It is an era that has always attracted poets and a smattering of novelists. The much-cited 1876 novel *Der Kampf um Rom* ('The Fight for Rome') by Felix Dahn is set in the first half of the sixth century. Despite its huge popularity, wild success and continuing availability, I must confess I fail to see its charms. Its 750 plodding pages have beaten me on several occasions. But the last few years have seen the later Roman Empire as a theme of films, books and computer games. The 2004 Antoine Fuqua-directed film *King Arthur* and the 2007 Doug Leffler film *The Last Legion* both have explicitly late Roman themes, the latter a fantasy on Romulus himself (they are both discussed in the final chapter of this book), while the latest addition to the immensely successful *Rome: Total War* computer game series is set around the barbarian invasions. There is increasingly a recognition among the public that this is a period in its own right.

The third aim of the book is to make the case that 476 was important. It may seem arrogant almost to the point of lunacy to take the stand against some of late antiquity's greatest historians. To pick just three of the naysayers, John Bury wrote that 'no empire fell in 476, there was no western empire to fall'; Averil Cameron has described Romulus' abdication as 'the most famous non-event in history'; Brian Croke calls it a manufactured turning point.[5]

Which also brings me to the title. If it seems provocative, it is deliberately so. Valid arguments could be made for half a dozen roughly contemporary figures as being the last Roman. Ambrosius Aurelianus, the last Roman leader in Britain; Syagrius, the last military commander in Gaul; generals Flavius Aetius who saved the West from Attila and his colleague Count Boniface, governor of Africa. A recent biography of Justinian, the great sixth-century Byzantine emperor, is subtitled 'The Last Roman'. Finally, a case could be made for Julius Nepos, Romulus' predecessor, who strictly speaking was the last legal emperor.

There is a real danger, however, of playing down the events of 476. If the year seems arbitrary, in one sense it is. The need to mark events with a specific date, indeed the fact of its common usage, gives it an authority of its own. It does not matter that it is artificial. It is a vital marker, the boundary between the classical and medieval world. Romulus Augustulus might be a symbol, but, as many have recognised, symbols can often be more useful than facts. Of course like most frontiers, Romulus Augustulus' deposition is a slightly porous boundary. There is a vocal German tradition, for example, that dates the fall of the Western empire to 488, when Romulus' successor was himself supplanted by the Goths, and a case can be made for pretty much any time between the battle of Adrianople in 378 to the Byzantine capture of the Italian capital of Ravenna in 540.

But it is not enough to argue for Romulus' importance from the point of common usage, its canonisation, if you will. *The Last Roman* argues not just that something changed in AD 476, but that it was felt to have changed. The empire had been declining for decades, some would say centuries. Certainly, different Roman provinces declined at different rates. The collapse in Britain, separated from Rome both by distance and the English Channel, was much more dramatic than, say, that in the south of France. There was no single moment. But 476 was what the sociologist and journalist Malcolm Gladwell would call a tipping point – a pivotal event after which it became impossible to return to the previous status quo. No matter how young he was, how little he affected his citizens or even how faint a historical footprint he left, Romulus Augustulus was the last Roman emperor. It was the end of autonomous Roman rule in the West. When he was forced into retirement, the baubles of imperial rule left Rome. Although Italy's new leaders continued to wear a toga for a few more years, they emerged as new types of rulers.

The idea of decline had become so contagious by the time Romulus was placed on the throne that it had become a self-fulfilling prophecy. The difficulty that historians have with 476 is that there was no impressive invasion nor were there massed ranks of barbarians storming a citadel. There was no overthrow, as one of the first modern British historians to look at the period points out, of the national polity such as happened with William the Conqueror's invasion of England in 1066 or of an existing order by a demagogic force as in the French Revolution.[6] The events that Romulus Augustulus' deposition most resembles are the shuffling off of Bahadur Shah, the last Mughal emperor of Delhi, retired to Burma by the British in 1858, or Tokugawa Yoshinobu, the last Japanese shogun, sidelined by the Meiji restoration a decade later.

Late antiquity poses a number of problems for the historian. It is an uncomfortable era of history to categorise. Is it late Roman history? Is it early modern history? Where exactly should we place it? It is not quite classical and not nearly medieval enough. None of this has been helped by the academic profession itself. The division between classics and history has long remained marked with a suspicion of dilettantism for anyone interested in both. Until recently, this had changed little since the eighteenth century and time of Edward Gibbon, who remarked that the period was faintly marked by obscure names and imperfect annals. Glasgow University Library, where I read, for example, is typical. Books on the subject are split between classics, theology and modern history on floor eight and floor ten. Practical frustrations aside, they still point to a general perception that the late Roman Empire is 'a corpse to be dragged quickly offstage so that the next great act of the drama of the Middle Ages should begin'.[7]

A detailed analysis of the collapse of the Roman Empire is beyond the scope of this volume. It took Edward Gibbon nine volumes to come to his conclusions, while more recently one German academic has identified 210 reasons for its decline (a conclusion that says as much about German historiography as it does about the collapse of the Roman Empire). Even the most recent, and by far the most readable history of the empire's decline, Peter Heather's *Fall of the Roman Empire*, comes in at over 500 pages.

The Last Roman takes for granted that the Roman Empire fell. Western Europe in AD 500 looked nothing like Western Europe in AD 400.

In itself this is a controversial statement, though thankfully not to the degree that it used to be. Until recently it had become a modern historical trope to claim that nothing that much changed after the fall of the empire. For most people it was business as usual. Romulus Augustulus is nothing more than an interesting footnote, went the argument, and the Roman West evolved or grew up rather than vanished. The most significant proponent of this view has been Peter Brown. His immensely successful *The World of Late Antiquity*, published in 1971 – in which Romulus is not worthy even of a name check – was the first popular view of the Roman Empire properly to challenge head-on the old school view of the decline and fall. He emphasised the themes of restructuring and transformation, of change and continuity over violent upheaval. The *reductio ad absurdam* of this school of thought was reached in a book called *Barbarians and Romans AD 418–584*. Its subtitle ('The techniques of accommodation') tells you as much as you need to know.

This theory, charmingly characterised by one historian as the 'tea party at the Roman vicarage' theory of settlement by invitation, is now thankfully losing ground.[8] Two academic giants in the field of late antiquity, Bryan Ward-Perkins and Peter Heather, have in recent years sounded clarion calls revising this impression of the end of the empire as one of peaceful transition. They both argue that the decline of Rome from the mid-fourth century onwards led to a collapse of society so dramatic that the result really was the end of civilisation. It was violent, it was unpleasant, it was brutal. As the art historian Kenneth Clark memorably opined at the beginning of his landmark television series *Civilisation*: 'For two centuries the heart of European civilisation almost stopped beating.'

Four snapshots, from four different parts of the Western empire and by those who were close to the events, should suffice to indicate the permanent sense of physical danger that faced individual Romans. By the middle of the fifth century, imperial grip on the province of Noricum, roughly the modern country of Austria, was loosening. Writing at the very beginning of the sixth century, the monk Eugippius is an important character because he is the first Western writer to acknowledge the day-to-day fall of the Roman Empire. His biography of St Severinus, who lived for much of his life in the region, is discussed in Chapter 3 for the light it sheds on Romulus Augustulus and his family. But the saint's repeated warnings about the 'sudden and heavy disaster' of barbarian invasions about to befall Noricum echo throughout the period. One of the most moving anecdotes he relates, precisely because the account of it is so casual, is of the janitor of the monastery at Mautern and his assistant, who leave the safety of the city walls at midday to gather fruit. Within sight of the city, only a couple of miles from its walls, they are kidnapped by barbarian raiders.[9] Rome could no longer guarantee its citizens' protection even in daylight.

Around the same time in France, the city of Clermont was besieged year after year by the Visigoths. There was no point in planting crops if one could not guarantee a harvest, and so famine hit the town. One reads the account of Sidonius Apollinaris with an ironic grimace. In what was, many centuries later, to be the home both of Michelin and its eponymous guide, the town's bishop writes of people tearing grasses from the crannies in the walls to eat, plucking at them 'with livid hands of starvation'. Their pallor, he notes, was hardly less green than the weeds they were trying to eat.[10] The famous *pax Romana* was well and truly buried.

The fifth-century bishop, political activist and chronicler Hydatius, in what is now northern Portugal, laments the shrinking frontiers of a Roman Empire that is 'doomed to perish'. His chronicle, written in the late AD 460s is a depressing account of battles lost, treachery and murder. He describes plundering, pestilence and, most unpleasant of all, mothers forced by hunger to eat their children. His account is embellished, but there is no mistaking the hatred in his words when he mentions that the survivors of these onslaughts had to live under Germanic rule, under 'barbarian slavery'.[11]

In Britain, Gildas, the first man in the entire West to write a provincial history, paints a similarly apocalyptic picture of a Britain abandoned by Rome and under Saxon assault.[12] Writing just over a century after the departure of the last legionaries he describes the destruction of the country in the mid-fifth century. All major towns were attacked, towers were torn down and walls were breached. The human cost in the face of the barbarian attacks was huge. He describes dismembered corpses, crusted over with purple blood that looked as though they had been mixed up in a terrible wine-press. These victims found no graves; the only burial that these unfortunates had, he says, were in the wreckage of houses and the bellies of animals and birds.

In the face of this onslaught the wretched survivors fled for mainland Europe and Ireland, escaping Britain as best they could. Gildas has them singing one of the Psalms as they left: 'Thou hast given us like sheep appointed for meat/ and hast scattered us among the heathen'.[13]

It is commonplace to nod sagely at these descriptions and to discard them as rhetorical exaggerations. But many of these accounts of decline are corroborated by archaeology. In Britain, for example, gone were the tiles and bricks of Roman construction. Instead, people had to make do with much less permanent structures. Two attempts to construct buildings in the old style, Benedict Biscop's churches of St Paul's in Jarrow and St Peter's in Monkwearmouth in the north of England in the 670s and 680s, feel cramped and small, almost like bad artists' impressions of the real thing. It is deeply unfashionable to make any kind of qualitative judgement when looking at art from different cultures and periods, but it does not require too attuned an aesthetic sensibility to see that these bear no comparison to such fifth-century buildings as the church of Santa Sabina in Rome or that of San Giovanni Evangelista in Ravenna.

Even Rome herself, while not showing as extreme or as dramatic a decline as elsewhere in the empire, had a distinctly tatty feel to it. Throughout the fifth century the population of the city nosedived and the city's infrastructure crumbled. There are no records of any civic building repairs from the reign of Emperor Honorius at the start of the century until the reign of Theoderic at the end (and discussed in Chapter 4). By 440 the situation had become so critical that Emperor Valentinian III commanded the people of Rome to fix the aqueducts and patch up the buildings themselves. In the Italian countryside, the picture was even worse. South Etruria had lost almost four-fifths of its rural sites by AD 500.[14]

Perhaps the most immediate archaeological symbol of collapse are the artefacts from around the dinner table. Throughout the empire, Roman chefs such as Apicius had at their disposal an entire *batterie de cuisine*. An element of variety is seen not just in mansions in Rome, but even in the most rural of houses. By the seventh century all that remained was a series of basic shapes, most common of which was a squat cooking pot that was used for everything.[15] There is a massive difference between a society that has time to eat for pleasure and one that eats for survival.

It is not just the case that provinces of the empire declined at different rates. The difficulty, as Jill Harries insightfully points out, is that the fall of the Roman Empire meant different things to different people. Inevitably, those reporting events are focused on the ways that the collapse affected them personally. For Severinus in Austria it meant the loss of the military; for Hydatius in

Portugal and Gildas in Britain it was characterised by the terrible state of the Church and the moral decline of society; for Sidonius Apollinaris, it meant the collapse of the political professional world in which he had been brought up to believe.

What unifies all these accounts are images of poverty, physical danger and uncertainty. As significant is what they do not offer. There is no indication that the situation can be reversed. Hope was dying in the West. 'In the past the Romans were the most powerful, now we have no strength. They were feared; now it is we who are fearful. Barbarous nations paid tribute to them, but to these same nations they are now tributary.' When the Christian writer Salvian of Marseilles wrote these gloomy words in the 440s he was not prophesying some future apocalyptic event, he was commenting on the here and now.[16] By the time of Romulus, there was no chance whatsoever of going back. You can search fifth-century writers in vain for reports of attempted imperial restoration. However much individual elements of *Romanitas* might struggle on, the empire had fallen.

My own favourite analogy for the fall appears in the fifth elegy of a little-known sixth-century Roman elegiac poet called Maximian the Etruscan – to the best of my knowledge he has never been translated into English. A younger contemporary of the philosopher and writer Boethius, he was famous as a lawyer and orator as well as a poet. On a business trip to Constantinople, a diplomatic mission for the Gothic king Theoderic, he movingly relates how the attractions of a young lady, possibly his landlady, distracted him from matters political. At the crucial moment, despite her enthusiastic ministrations, he found himself unable to rise to the occasion. He blamed old age and infirmity.

It is hard to think of a more apposite metaphor for the flagging powers of the West.

*   *   *

It has become commonplace to write that there are few sources for late antiquity. Many echo the comment of the fifth-century writer and bishop Sidonius Apollinaris who wrote that 'one might almost speak of literature as dead and buried'.[17] It is true that for most Greek and Roman history, it is often just a case of reaching for the red or green Loeb volumes of translated Latin and Greek writers respectively, supplemented, if necessary, by the French Budé editions of the classical canon. It is also fair to say that from the end of the fourth century onwards the task becomes much more difficult. The Loeb Classical Library covers the fifth century only intermittently, while Penguin Classics, normally the first stop for the interested general reader, has editions of only a couple of the writers that will appear in these pages.

Great steps have been taken by, for example, the Liverpool University Press with its 'Translated Texts for Historians' series of volumes. Since 1985 it has allowed a great number of the voices of late antiquity to speak in English for the first time. Nonetheless, a great number of primary sources for the period still remain in the decent obscurity of their original language. There is no English translation of many of the writings of Ennodius, the poems of Maximian have been rendered into German, but not English, and there has never been a complete translation of the letters of Cassiodorus into English. Despite a wonderful edition in 1992 by S.J.B. Barnish, the fullest translation so far remains Thomas Hodgkin's from 1886.

With earlier Roman history it is not normally necessary to introduce the sources used for events. For the first chapter of the book we are, for the most part, in the safe and familiar hands of fourth-century writers. Ammianus Marcellinus, St Augustine and St Jerome are fairly well known, and translations of their writings are easily available. But it is worth taking a moment to introduce the men through whose eyes we are able to discern something of the fifth century. It is by no means a complete list, but it gives a sense of the range of people and types of sources we are talking about.

The best known perhaps is the Byzantine historian Procopius. Few who have read his account of the Empress Theodora's early career as a call girl and her specialised performance with geese in *The Secret History* can ever fully erase the memory. Born in Caesarea Maritima on the coast of Palestine in around 500, he trained as a lawyer in Byzantium before, in his late 20s, becoming private secretary to the great general Flavius Belisarius. Several of his works survive, most pertinently, his *History of the Wars*, which covers the reign of Romulus Augustulus and the aftermath in some depth.

Eugippius and Ennodius are perhaps the most overlooked writers. Eugippius, mentioned earlier, was a churchman and friend probably to Romulus Augustulus, certainly to his mother and father. His biography of St Severinus, written in around 511, shines a spotlight on provincial society in decline. Magnus Felix Ennodius is another churchman, bishop of Pavia, whose writings reflect life in northern Italy up to the reign of Theoderic. While there have been several English editions of Eugippius' *Life of St Severinus* and Ennodius' *Life of St Epiphanius*, both the latter's panegyric to Theoderic and his letters remain untranslated.

The landowner, bishop, politician, writer Sidonius Apollinaris is an unparalleled source for the collapse of the West. In the 147 letters of his which have survived and were published in the late 470s, the bishop of Clermont reveals how the Gallo-Roman aristocracy achieved compromise with the barbarians; how, despite doubts, they recognised and found accommodation with them.

As one modern historian points out: 'If Cassiodorus had been a contemporary of Tacitus, the *Variae* would be required reading in every classical department in the world.'[18] Born only a few years after Romulus had been deposed (sometime in the 480s) into an aristocratic family in southern Italy, he rose to become Theoderic's private secretary and, under his successors, head of the civil service. Hundreds of his professional letters survive, some 486 of them dating to between 506 and 538, and gathered together in the *Variae*, a collection he put together after his retirement. As for the letters themselves, it is true to say that they exhibit an element of style over content. So allusive are they, that they read, at times, like a cryptic crossword. But he is important for what can be seen as an apology for Theoderic's Gothic regime and for the Roman aristocracy that collaborated with it.

Jordanes was a bishop writing in Latin, in Byzantium in the very early 550s. He was originally a civil servant from a Germanic family, and two of his works survive: the *Romana*, a brief history of the Roman world, which to the best of my knowledge remains untranslated, and the *Getica*, sometimes known in English as *The Origin and Deeds of the Goths*. His perspective is important because there is no doubt in his mind that the Roman Empire is finished. 'By now you should know how the Roman Empire began, how it grew, how it subjected the whole world to its sway, and how it lost the world again under inept leadership', is how he concludes the *Romana*. Both books are infused with a profound sense of loss; *Romana* for a faded Rome trying and failing to make the best of it, the *Getica* for a Gothic Empire, that of his people, defeated.[19]

Finally it is worth commenting on a specific type of historical writing called the chronicles, increasingly being regarded as a literary genre in their own right. These are, as the name suggests, accounts of events and years, often with details that do not occur elsewhere. Several feature in the following pages, but two should be singled out. The first is called the *Anonymous Valesianus* or the *Excerpta Valesiana*. In fact it is by two writers, separated by a century, who only come under a single heading because they were published in Paris by Henri de Valois in 1636. The first half was written in 390 and is a biography of Constantine the Great; the second half, which concerns us here, was written in 550 and covers the period from 474 to 526. The second chronicler, Count Marcellinus, we have already met. Although he spent his life at the court of Byzantium, he wrote in Latin. His chronicle covers the period from 379 to 534, when he died.

A few brief notes at the end. All translations are my own unless otherwise indicated. For those who wish to read the sources in the original or in another edition, it is normal practice to follow the convention in the notes of giving the name of the author, the work and then chapter and section number. In cases where this might cause confusion or where modern scholarship has renumbered passages, I have also added page numbers. As for cities and towns, modern anglicised names have been used throughout unless the old ones are better known. In a similar vein all proper names have been harmonised too, so although Romulus Augustulus' successor can at times appears as Odoacer and Odoaker, here he remains Odovacer.

The most enjoyable part of a project such as this is to thank those who have been generous with their time and expertise to help me. I am only now beginning to appreciate what Sam Barnish tried to teach me many years ago. Special thanks to Winder McConnell, Opritsa Popa, Giovanna Raffone, Melody Monfreda, Andrew Pleavin, Joshua Friedman, Mike Aquilina and the Ravenna Tourist Office. All have been extremely generous with their advice and help. I have also benefited from the help of Ilona Gymer, Alan Murdoch, Carrie Quinlan, Denis Pritchard and Vernon Baxter. As ever, I cannot begin to thank John Hatfield enough for his comments and encouragement on the draft manuscript. I am hugely fortunate to be able to count him both a colleague and a friend. Christopher Feeney and Jane Entrican at Sutton Publishing have been unfailingly helpful, as have the staff of Glasgow University Library. Finally, the book would be lost without the scalpel precision of editor Alison Miles.

I have been very lucky in my last two books to profit from the guidance of my father, Brian Murdoch. For the first time, however, our interests have overlapped and I have been able to benefit properly from his many years of scholarship. It has been a great pleasure to sit on his shoulders.

All mistakes, of course, remain my own.

As ever, I would like to thank, for her support and enthusiasm, my wife Susy, to whom this book is dedicated, with love.

ONE

Guess Who's Coming to Dinner?

For three days from 24 August 410, the unthinkable happened. Rome was conquered by barbarians. 'A dreadful rumour reaches us from the west. Rome is occupied . . . My voice is choked with sobs as I dictate these words. The city that conquered the universe is herself conquered,' writes St Jerome.[1]

The Gothic king Alaric had marched on the city. It was his third attempt on Rome and this time it worked. All the gates had been blocked and the port was isolated. The heart of the Roman Empire could expect little help from Ravenna, where the 26-year-old Emperor Honorius had hidden with his court for the last eight years. He was not exactly the figurehead the empire needed at a time like this.

Traditionally there are two rival accounts of the capture of the city. One has it that Rome, blockaded, besieged and already in the grip of cannibalism, was betrayed by a female aristocrat who ordered her servants to open the city's gates at night. The other has it that Alaric had picked out 300 young men from his army. These he had pretended to give as slaves to members of the Roman nobility. Once they had gained their masters' trust, they waited until noon on the fixed day and then opened the Salarian Gate in the north-east of the city – at which point the Goths stormed the city.[2]

In fact there was little need for treachery. Famine, the siege and the disease caused by festering, putrid corpses that could not be buried outside the city walls had sapped Rome of the will to fight.

The city was burned, robbed and plundered. One Byzantine historian mentions the house of the great Republican historian Sallust, which had managed to survive most of the empire, but was burned as the city was taken. Writing over a century later he claimed that its charred timbers could still be seen, a constant reminder of the disaster.

Was the sack as bad as people said? Most writers both then and now claim that it could have been a great deal worse. Alaric apparently ordered that if anyone were to take refuge in a church or shrine, especially in the basilicas of the holy Apostles Peter and Paul, both they and the buildings should remain unharmed and unmolested. Rome at the end of the fifth century could still boast eighty gilded and sixty-four ivory statues of pagan gods. The account of the Portuguese theologian Paulus Orosius is one of the more interesting, specifically because he tries to downplay events. His book, the *History against the Pagans*, is an attempt to show that the sack of Rome was not as bad as all that and that life had been worse for Christians in the past, under the Emperor Nero for example.[3]

His report is not entirely convincing though. At times his argument would seem to propose that it is better to be shot by firing squad than to be hanged. In contrast, one historian writes that Alaric 'allowed each of his followers to seize as much Roman wealth as he could and to plunder all the houses'. And individual accounts of casual violence point away from the gentlemanly sack that some suggest. An elderly lady, a friend of St Jerome's, was beaten up when she denied having any treasure in her house. She died a few days afterwards.[4]

Locust-like, the Goths left as quickly as they had arrived. Three days after entering Rome, they departed. But reaction to the devastation was one of absolute shock. All parts of the empire were affected as refugees fled Italy. Jerome in Palestine commented that there were no parts of the earth where the

Romans were not in exile. The whole of the East, of Egypt, of Africa was full of refugees, he says. Even his own monastery had become a hostel. 'All we can do is to sympathise and unite our tears with theirs,' he writes sadly.[5]

While Jerome's theology was always better than his political analysis, it is fair to say that the psychological damage inflicted by the sack of Rome was greater than the material disaster. The question to which Christian writers at the time kept returning was why had God allowed the Goths to pillage the city? It was, without doubt, a period of soul-searching, and numerous theologians attempted to portray it as a harbinger of the apocalypse. This emoting reached its apotheosis, albeit a long-winded one, in St Augustine's theological masterpiece *City of God*, one of the great cornerstones of Western European thought.

The questions remain: how did Rome get to this state? How did the city that had conquered the world, that still remains the measure for empire, become ruled by childish and childlike emperors and plagued by barbarian invaders?

The beginning of the end was the battle of Adrianople on 9 August 378. At least that is how Roman contemporaries, and many historians today, saw it. The 1924 *Cambridge Medieval History* calls it 'the last act of the great drama'. It is also where the fourth-century writer Ammianus Marcellinus, the last of Rome's great historians in the traditions of Livy and Tacitus, for example, finishes his history of the Roman world.[6]

No one will ever know whether it was arrogance or incompetence – it was probably a mixture of both – but for the Romans, the battle was a military catastrophe from the outset. The 50-year-old emperor Valens, a cruel and boorish man who was particularly sensitive to *lèse-majesté*, took the field against the Goths near what is now the dusty Turkish town of Edirne, close to the borders of Greece and Bulgaria. He could not bear to wait for military assistance from his younger nephew, Gratian, emperor of the West.

Army intelligence was conspicuous by its absence. Valens, hugely underestimating the size of the Gothic army, believed that there was no need to compromise with their forces as he was likely to win. On the day itself, matters were not helped by the fact that he had marched out first thing in the morning. By the time the emperor took the field facing the Goths, who had camped on top of a hill, on a blistering hot afternoon, his soldiers were already tired, thirsty and hungry. Neither their physical nor their mental state were helped by smoke from the fields that the Goths had burned to delay and distract them.

Ammianus' account is horrible:[7]

Then the two lines of battle dashed against each other, like the prows of ships, and thrusting with all their might, were tossed here and there, like the waves of the sea. Our left wing had advanced actually up to the Gothic wagons, and they would have pushed still further if they had received proper support. But they were abandoned by the rest of the cavalry. Pressed by the numbers of the enemy, they were knocked down and collapsed like the ruin of a vast rampart. Our infantry was left unprotected and the different units huddled together so that a soldier could barely draw his sword or had room to move his hand. Such clouds of dust arose that it was almost impossible to see the sky, which resounded with horrible cries. As a result, enemy missiles, which were bearing death on every side, found their mark, and fell with deadly effect.

By the evening, it was all over. Almost in shock the old historian writes that two-thirds of the soldiers, some 10,000 men, were killed and the emperor himself not only lost his life, but his body was never recovered. Many accounts report that Valens was burned to death in a hut where he was hiding out. Ammianus also makes a point of mentioning the number of senior commanders that were killed. 'No battle in our history except Cannae was such a massacre', he notes, comparing the defeat to Hannibal's massacre of the Roman army in 216 BC, which was the literary benchmark for defeat.[8]

It does not matter that the feared Gothic attack on Constantinople fizzled out (they were discouraged, claims Ammianus, at the sight of the city's walls[9]) and the Goths dispersed. Nor that in reality this was no repeat of Cannae. But like the sack of Rome, it was much more significant as a psychological setback than as a military defeat. The empire had not only seen two major defeats within a decade, but it had lost two emperors in doing so – Julian the Apostate had been killed in battle with Persia, fifteen years previously. Much like young Victorians paralysed in disbelief by news of defeats in the Boer War, Rome found it hard to grasp that the Roman military machine was no longer invincible.

Little wonder that the event encouraged others to flights of apocalyptic fancy. Ambrose, bishop of Milan, writing a month after the event, believed that he had witnessed: 'the destruction of the entire globe, the end of the world, the funerals of relatives, the deaths of fellow citizens', and, above all, 'the violation of holy virgins and widows'. Libanius, Antiochene friend of the Emperor Julian and arch-pagan, is scarcely less doom-laden. 'Until now the Goths used to shiver every time they heard mention of Roman skill in warfare, but now they are victorious and we die, nobly and as befits brave men, but perishing all the same.'[10]

And it was the Goths who had been the first new entrants into the empire. In the summer of 376, they stood on the banks of the Danube and, in the words of the Greek sophist and historian Eunapius, 'stretched out their hands from afar with cries and lamentations begging for pity and asking to be allowed to cross'. In reality of course they were by no means the first. There had been trickles of barbarians into the empire since the days of the early principate. It had always been an efficient method of getting new bodies into the army and a convenient new source of tax revenues. But this was different. Ammianus Marcellinus writes: 'to try to find their number is as vain as counting the wind-swept Libyan sands'.[11]

The blame for the appearance of the Goths was laid at the feet of the Huns. It is difficult to perceive the origins of these mysterious barbarians from the East, Eurasian nomads who had come into Europe, riding along the north coast of the Black Sea. It is often said that they are related to the Hiung-Nu against whom the Great Wall of China was built, but lack of evidence, prejudice and legend make it unlikely that a definitive answer can ever be found. Their presence was felt, rather than seen. Ammianus Marcellinus' account, second-hand of course, is a mixture of exaggeration and invective. They are short, stumpy and scarred, unhygienic (there is the nose-wrinkling detail that they only removed shirts when they disintegrated) and of course incredible horsemen and archers. Jerome, who can always be counted on to be less than measured, writes of the descent of the 'northern wolves' and rivers running with blood.[12] While the direct cause and effect between the arrival of the Huns in Europe and that of the Goths knocking at the door of the Roman Empire has now been largely rejected, there is no doubt that they were a factor of encouragement.

In the beginning it is fair to agree with those who see a more gentle process, what Peter Brown calls 'a gold rush' rather than an invasion of barbarians. It should not be forgotten that they were expressly invited in. Emperor Valens was distracted by campaigns in the East against Persia and viewed these Goths as potential recruits for his army. The growing Roman lack of enthusiasm for military service is hard to overestimate. New recruits were often locked up to stop them trying to escape, and by September 381 a law had been passed making it illegal to avoid military service by amputating your own fingers. The penalty was branding and then service anyway. If people were prepared to mutilate themselves rather than join up, little wonder that Valens was prepared to accommodate the barbarians.[13]

The barbarian movements were pretty much peaceful and contained, at least initially. The difficulties that began to emerge were the result of greater numbers than expected seeking sanctuary. That in turn led to food shortages. The exploitation of these asylum seekers by the Romans in charge of monitoring the Goths, at a grass-roots level, was jaw-droppingly insensitive. So desperate were they for food that one account records the Romans swapping dogs for Gothic children. The children were sold into slavery; the dogs became supper.[14]

Continued food shortages triggered the Gothic rebellion that climaxed with the Roman defeat at Adrianople. Low-grade conflict persisted for the next four years, resulting in the loss of the Balkans, until peace between the Goths and the Romans was finally signed in October 382, by Valens' successor, the vastly talented 33-year-old Theodosius. An experienced soldier from a military family, he was the polar opposite of his inept predecessor. Nonetheless, the treaty that Theodosius inked was another moment of no return. If the battle of Adrianople had been the encouragement to the top of the slide, then the peace treaty was the Romans starting to push themselves down.

First and foremost, although presented by Roman historians as a Gothic surrender, the accord's terms were suspiciously and untypically generous. As Peter Heather writes: 'the absence of revenge, punishment and example-setting . . . is extraordinary'.[15] In return for serving as auxiliaries in the Roman army (under their own commanders) the Goths were given land, settled as a distinct ethnic group on Roman territory and made exempt from taxes. The cherry on top of the icing was that they were responsible for their own defence. This was momentous. No emperor had gone this far before in giving barbarians autonomy. Rome was devolving its power.

The imperial propaganda machine moved swiftly to quell any public doubts about the wisdom of such a move. One orator asked whether it was better to 'fill Thrace with corpses or with farmers? Is it better to show it filled with graves or with men? Is it better to walk through empty lands or cultivated fields.' It was a theme that Roman rhetoricians had a chance to warm to. Another, speaking in the Senate House in Rome in front of the emperor, his staff and the senate in mid-389 said that it was a smart move to let in the barbarians 'to supply soldiers for your camps and farmers for our lands'. He went on to say: 'Whatever barbarian nation was ever a menace to us because of its strength, ferocity or numbers either thinks it a good idea not to disturb the peace, or else if it is subservient, rejoices as if well-disposed towards us.' Swords into ploughshares indeed.[16]

But what no number of speeches could do was to paper over the deep and ingrained Roman suspicion of the barbarian. They were always a collective other. What would nowadays be categorised as racism is considerably more complex than that. The defeated barbarian had been a part of Rome's self-image for centuries – think of the number of skewered barbarians depicted on funeral monuments and coins for example. Any barbarian integration was only superficial, and Rome was certainly swift to fight back if there was any trouble. After the battle of Adrianople, many Goths in Roman custody were simply murdered. After a later victory over the Goths at the start of the fifth century, the captives were sold 'like the cheapest cattle' for a gold coin each.[17]

These, admittedly extreme, examples are just the tip of the anti-barbarian iceberg, but they indicate consistent and endemic Roman reserve towards the barbarian. However much barbarians might want to ape Roman society there was an impassable bridge between them and civilisation. In the 470s Sidonius Apollinaris could cruelly mock a friend who had bothered to learn the Burgundian native language ('You can hardly conceive how amused we all are to hear,' he writes). As late as the end of the sixth century Gregory the Great noted that the difference between barbarian and Roman rule was that the former were lords of slaves while the latter were lords of free men.[18]

As if ethnicity were not enough, the differences between barbarians and the Romans were further underscored by their religious beliefs. The Romans were Catholic, the Goths were Arians. This brand of Christianity was named after the early fourth-century priest Arius, who argued that although both were divine, God the father was superior to, rather than the equal of, Jesus. Arianism had become the Gothic orthodoxy in the mid-fourth century following work north of the Danube by the missionary bishop Ulfila. He had converted them, given them an alphabet and allegedly translated the entire Bible into Gothic (with the exception of the Book of Kings, which he deemed too bloody). For reasons of complexity as much as space, religion is a theme alluded to rather than addressed in this volume, but it should be borne in mind as a continuous baseline throughout the period.

Allowing the Goths to cross the River Danube proved to be the breach in the wall of the Roman Empire, but of course it did not signal a collapse, at least not quite yet. It is easy to forget that for many citizens the fourth century was a time of growth and expansion. This was true even on the Danube frontier. Forts along the river such as Novae, Iatrus (Krivina) and Abritus (Razgrad) expanded, as did manufacturing, both of arms and civilian industries, and circulation of coins increased too. Take the headquarters of Legion I 'Italian' at Novae, now Svishtov in Bulgaria, which controlled one of the easiest and most popular crossings of the Danube. There was significant remodelling in the fourth century (extensive fortifications can still be seen today), the construction of U-shaped towers that were spaced to allow overlapping fields of fire from archers and ballistae.[19]

What turned the breach into a flood was the unexpected death of Emperor Theodosius in Milan on 17 January 395. The empire was then split between his two sons, Arcadius, in the East and Honorius in the West. They were 18 and 10 respectively, though alike in their general incompetence. A surviving cameo of Honorius displays a weak and arrogant character and rumours of his overly familiar relationship with his sister speak volumes of what people thought of him.[20] Although one of Theodosius' great successes is that he founded a dynasty that was to run for the next fifty-five years, the youth of the two boys heralded the other great portent of the decline of the West, the shift in power from the emperors to the generals. If the collapse of the Roman Empire was accelerated by barbarian pressure, it was also helped along by the weakening role of the emperor as a series of brilliant military men took over the reins of power.

There was no question that Honorius was too young to rule on his own. In his place as commander-in-chief, as guardian and as the Roman Empire's ruler sat Flavius Stilicho. A fascinating, much-debated figure who managed to keep his grip on power for over a decade, his character remains elusive. Appointed by Theodosius to look after his son, Stilicho was notable for several reasons, above all because he was what the Romans called *semibarbarus*.[21] His father was a Vandal – he had been a highly decorated barbarian cavalry officer – and his mother was a Roman. It is possible to get a sense of his barbarian/Roman heredity in the best-known image of him, an ivory diptych in the cathedral treasury in Monza. The technique and materials are undeniably Roman; the image is distinctly barbarian.

Stilicho's authority came from the imperial royal family. The fact that he had been appointed as what was in essence regent and had married Serena, the former emperor's niece and adopted daughter, made him untouchable. A recognition of this lay behind his encouraging Honorius to marry his daughter. Bound so tightly to the Theodosian memory, no one would dare set themselves up against him. Authority, however, was not enough. The final piece in the jigsaw was power, and Stilicho's strength was drawn from the army.

Over time, this coincidence of power – a young, weak emperor guided by a powerful military man – was encouraged. Stilicho himself began to move in this direction when in 402 he persuaded Honorius to move his capital from Milan to Ravenna for reasons of security during the invasions of Italy. The geographical division between Stilicho and his emperor underlined the political separation of powers. In coins, for example, emperors are increasingly portrayed on coins as civilian figures. The dual nature of power between the military and the ceremonial was gradually refined over the next eighty years, reaching what with hindsight seems to be a logical conclusion when the roles of titular and actual head were split between Romulus Augustulus and his father Orestes.

Stilicho's title was that of patrician. Like many honorifics in late antiquity, the term is difficult to define. There is an inherent vagueness even in the writings of contemporary historians about people's rank, and this blurring is mirrored in inscriptions and laws. Throughout the book I have generally paraphrased rather than translated titles literally. Those like 'count of the sacred largesse', for example, are pretty meaningless to the general reader and distance them from the individual. A further challenge with the term patrician, however, is that it was also the title given as an honour, much like a life peerage in modern Britain, to leading civilians. Nonetheless, I have left the term as patrician in the hope that context makes it clear to which one I am referring.

With regard to Stilicho, several historians conventionally translate his position of patrician as generalissimo.[22] It does come close to giving the sense of a military commander who has the power to intervene in any civil matters he sees fit, though does not have the constitutional authority to do so. The closest parallel in the more modern world (especially in the light of its relationship with the monarchy) is that enjoyed by the shogunate which ruled Japan from the beginning of the seventeenth century until the mid-nineteenth century.

Stilicho had but a short time to enjoy his power since Theodosius' death had done little to preserve Rome's borders. The Goths took advantage of imperial distractions to revolt under their leader, Alaric, who had made his first appearance on the historical map the previous year (AD 394) as commander of Gothic auxiliary units in the service of the empire. Alaric was demanding official recognition. For his military help he wanted to be promoted to general. It was not until he had led his forces on a rampage through Greece that the Eastern empire crawled to the negotiating table. Once there, Eutropius, Stilicho's counterpart in the East, was able to deflect Alaric. He gave him the title he coveted and palmed him off on the West.

Alaric's first invasion of Italy left him with a bloody nose in Piedmont in April 402, but his defeat did not mean a let-up for Rome. The first decade of the fifth century saw a number of other major invasions in the West. The empire was to be allowed no chance to catch its breath. In 405 another large Gothic barbarian army invaded Italy. Although it was eventually defeated near Florence ('Without one casualty to Rome, without even one wounded,' claims St Augustine) it was the overture to a hard winter of discontent. On New Year's Eve 406, three tribes, Vandals, Alans and Suevi, breached the Rhine and ransacked Mainz before flooding into Gaul, down as far as Bordeaux and heading for Spain and Portugal at the end of the decade. Retrenching, the capital of Gaul was moved south from Trier to Arles. The effect of the invasions is summed up by the much-cited (though no less true for it) lines of Orientius, the bishop of Auch: 'In the villages and great villas, through the countryside, at crossroads, in every district, all along the roads – death, sorrow, suffering, fire and mourning. The whole of Gaul was filled with the smoke of a single funeral pyre.'[23]

That same year, Alaric received one of the strangest diplomatic overtures in history. Would he help Stilicho fight Constantinople? At first glance it beggars belief. It is easy to see why such a venture would appeal to Alaric, but what was in it for Stilicho? He could not, in all seriousness, have Eastern pretensions, could he? The most likely reason is not that he was planning an out-and-out assault against Byzantium itself, but rather that he needed to regain the territories of Dacia and parts of Illyricum, at the time under Constantinople's control. These had always proved to be good military recruiting grounds in the past and he desperately needed fresh troops to counter the Rhine breaches.[24] There are many reasons for the survival of the East and the collapse of the West, but that the recruiting grounds of the East were never threatened remains at the heart of Byzantium's continued existence. This agreement was to prove to be both Stilicho's own death warrant and another nail in the coffin of the empire.

The patrician and the Goth were distracted from Eastern ambitions by events in the West. To win at Florence, Stilicho had needed to mobilise a massive army. The effects of pulling reserve troops up to defend Italy hastened the end elsewhere in the empire. Britain spun off on its own. The withdrawal of a number of legions to save Italy threw up several pretenders to the imperial title in Britain, three in 407. The last and most successful of these, Constantine III, ruled for four years and made significant inroads in Continental Europe through Gaul before he was eventually murdered. No wonder that by 415 Jerome caricatured the island as 'a province fertile in tyrants'.[25]

For Stilicho, 407 disappeared in firefighting and 408 began no more optimistically. He was met with a demand for a cash advance from Alaric for expenses. It was that agreement to pay the Goth the not entirely unreasonable sum of 4,000lb of gold that sealed Stilicho's fate. The arrangement was deeply unpopular (one senator said 'this isn't peace but a deal for slavery'), and Stilicho was executed by what was in all but name a *coup d'état* on 22 August. As one modern historian has written: 'If the failure of Stilicho was a public tragedy, his personal tragedy was that he did not deserve to fail.' Many of his senior officers were wiped out too, and Honorius divorced Stilicho's daughter. Late Roman regime change was nothing if not thorough.[26]

In the autumn of 408, with Stilicho gone, there was nothing, or rather no one, to prevent Alaric's progress: and he aimed for Rome. It was the first of what were to be several assaults. Rather like a cat playing with a small bird, the Goth had at first no intention of taking the city. He wanted booty and still hoped for some kind of a treaty with Honorius. But after the failure of talks, Alaric returned to Rome to lay siege once more in 409. Finally fed up and frustrated, he sacked the city in 410.

The following years appear a slight anticlimax. There was no big finish and no attempt to set up a Gothic kingdom in Italy. Instead, Alaric decided to search for a Gothic homeland in Africa. But the fleet he built was destroyed in a storm and he died soon afterwards. His burial in a temporarily diverted riverbed, that of the River Busento near the city of Cosenza, was soon forgotten, and already by the time of Attila he had passed into semi-legend.

The Western empire spent the next fifteen years, up to the mid-420s, fighting off both revolutionary emperors and barbarians. The death of Honorius in August 423 sparked what by now was a familiar power struggle. It was not until October 425, and with the assistance of an Eastern army, that Honorius' 6-year-old nephew was proclaimed emperor. Nonetheless it took a further eight years for power fully to be consolidated. It goes without saying that the youthful Valentinian III had taken little part in the proceedings.

The real power behind the throne was the commander-in-chief of Gaul, Flavius Aetius. By 433, the general, who had been born in around 390, had seen off all other competitors for the role and had emerged as the true successor to Stilicho. His relationship with Valentinian III over the next twenty years went beyond that of Stilicho and Honorius, and as a refinement of power it was another step towards that of Romulus Augustulus and his father.

The writings of the general's contemporary, the late fourth-century historian Renatus Frigeridus, have sadly been lost, but his description of Aetius survives.[27] He was of medium height, had a lean physique, was 'manly and well-proportioned'. Aetius was a sound horseman, a good shot (a possible hangover from his youth in barbarian hands) and handy with a lance. If Stilicho had been able to draw on his barbarian heritage, Aetius was able to pull on the experience of having spent his childhood as a hostage first at the Gothic court of Alaric and then with the Huns.

His career had been stellar and it was recognised as such. A statue to him had been erected in an important public building in Rome around 440. The inscription, which survives, recounts his career and describes him as 'devoted to the Republic and decorated with every military honour'. A panegyric written by one of Aetius' deputies a couple of years later confirms the general mood of public adulation and gratitude: 'Your bed is a barren rock or a thin covering on the ground,' he writes. 'You spend your nights in watchfulness, your days in toil. And you undergo this hardship willingly. Your breastplate is not so much a defence as a normal item of clothing.'[28] Whatever the later criticism of Aetius, he had earned his position.

Aetius has been criticised for focusing initially on securing his own position rather than fighting barbarians. By the time he had finished doing so the army senior command were all Aetian loyalists, but as Peter Heather accurately points out, 'political crisis does not suspend personal ambition – in fact, it often gives rivalry an extra point'. It does not alter the fact that he did a great deal to stop parts of the empire spinning off. He did an incredible job, specifically in Gaul, clamping down on various assorted barbarians along with a hodge-podge of insurgents that comprised everything from genuine separatists to bandits (though in the sources they are lumped together by writers in late antiquity under the catch-all term Bagaudae). But Aetius also fought in territory that is now Belgium, Germany, Austria and Italy and recovered much of Spain. Little wonder then that from the perspective of the sixth century one historian could dub him 'the last of the Romans'.[29]

It is worth digressing for a moment to look at how the empire collapsed in Britain. The chronology of Britain in the fifth century is confusing in the extreme, which is partly why it has proved such fertile soil for legends. The academic literature is intimidatingly technical, minutely nuanced and consensus is unlikely.

At the turn of the century Britain remained very much part of the empire, though the last quarter of the fourth saw both recession and the abandonment of buildings. There was a general decline in standards in large towns, which can be seen in the breakdown of civic infrastructure. An unpleasant olfactory insight to this physical decline can be imagined with the collapse of the public sewage system in Canterbury. Militarily it was a similar story. The barbarian Rhine crossings needed the withdrawal of some troops from Britain, the final battalion from Hadrian's Wall. Stilicho's publicist, the poet Claudian, writes that 'there also came the legion set to guard the furthest Britons, the legion that curbs the savage Scot and scans the lifeless patterns tattooed on dying Picts'. The few remaining soldiers – we know some stayed at Housesteads and Chesterholm and several other forts along the wall – made the best of it they could.[30]

London had stopped minting British coinage by the late 380s, and the very last issues even to reach Britain from the Continent were those of Honorius and Arcadius. With no salaries, few were prepared to support the state for free. Britain soon fell prey to 'hungry and greedy wolves' – the Saxons who continued to attack throughout much of the second decade. There was to be no help from Rome against these 'blue-eyed' lords of the seas and their 'curved ships'. In 410 Emperor Honorius sent his famous letter, his rescript, advising Britain to 'look to its own security'. The *Chronicle of 452* (roughly) confirms the date. Typically briefly it just notes: 'In the 16th year of the reign of Honorius, the British provinces were devastated by an invasion of Saxons.'[31]

No sooner had the Romans withdrawn than Saxons were joined by Pictish and Scottish raiders too. In the unpleasant image of the sixth-century British bishop Gildas, they appeared 'like dark throngs of worms which in the heat of the midday sun come out of their narrow holes'. The huge numbers of coin hoards that have been found – well over sixty – indicate the general uncertainty. The sheen of civilisation was tarnished rapidly as society turned in on itself. While in Continental Europe individuals could still be referred to as Britons (the lid of a sarcophagus in Arles, dating to the mid-fifth century, records the epitaph of a certain Tolasanus, described as *Britannus Natione*) grave stones in Britain refer to local and tribal loyalties.[32]

There are numerous examples of the damage caused by the raiders, possibly the most affecting can be seen in the Yorkshire signal stations. These were a northern extension of the Forts of the Saxon Shore in south-east England (the best-preserved example can be seen at Burgh Castle) which were set up as a response to barbarian attempts to outflank Hadrian's Wall after the AD 390s. What was revealed by archaeologists reminds you that for all the talk of economic considerations and military imperatives, the collapse of the empire involved real people.

When they were examined, at the beginning of the last century, two of the signal stations, Huntcliffe and Goldsborough, told a shocking story. Huntcliffe had been burned down by marauders.

When archaeologists excavated, they found the remains of fourteen individuals, some as young as 2 or 3. All had been killed and dumped head-first down the well. At Goldsborough, the picture of violence was painted in even greater clarity. The body of one of the last defenders lay in the south-east corner of the tower. Stabbed, seemingly from behind, the short (he was only just over 5ft), thick-set man in his 40s had fallen across the fire as he died. A younger man lay nearby, his throat ripped out. Over him lay a large powerful dog, defending his master to the last. Both these events can be dated to the early fifth century, Huntcliffe by a coin of Arcadius, Goldsborough by a coin of his brother Honorius.[33]

Although some towns, such as St Albans, Cirencester and Winchester kept their end up, Britain suffered at the hands of the invaders. In the 440s, the northern part of the country had fallen to Scots and Picts. By the end of the decade Britain had written to Aetius to ask for help to 'beat back the people of the north' – but received none. One of the kings, usually called Vortigern, used the power vacuum created by the lack of Roman military to settle some Saxons on his territory. It was a disastrous move and the newcomers began to move against the locals in what is known as the Saxon revolt. The coin hoard at Patching in Sussex, which includes a coin dating to the 460s (and so was valued as an indicator of wealth rather than for its monetary value) was buried at this time of insecurity.[34]

Those who survived mounted a resistance, and through the historical fog we catch the briefest of glimpses of Ambrosius Aurelianus. Dubbed by Gildas 'the last of the Romans', he emerged as the leading Romano-British leader in southern Britain until the end of the fifth century, gaining the upper hand over these invaders. He is described as 'a gentleman' whose parents 'had worn the purple and were slain in it'. This aristocrat became a focus of a Romano-British revival after the Saxon storm. 'Under him our people regained their strength, and challenged the victors to battle', writes the monk Gildas enthusiastically.[35]

By the end of the century, at some point in the last decade, the battle of Badon Hill took place in an unknown location in southern Britain. The significance of this event for most people is its connection with the myth of King Arthur. 'Gildas not only fails to acknowledge Arthur as a champion of the British cause, he does not mention Arthur in the *Ruin of Britain* at all,' warns one modern historian. Yet in both Nennius' *British History* and the *Welsh Annals*, it is the northern leader Arthur (the references to him in Nennius have a strong connection with Northumberland) who is given credit. By the twelfth century, an Aurelius Ambrosius is a brother of Uther Pendragon, while Merlin's second name is given as Ambrosius. The process of sidelining Ambrosius was complete. The tradition of Arthur dominates, that of Ambrosius ended up forgotten.[36]

Back in Rome, the economy that Aetius inherited was not, to put it mildly, in great shape. However much locals rationalised and accepted barbarians living on their land, no Roman would say that it was the best possible scenario. It did not matter whether it was military conquest or invasion by treaty, every one of the new settlers was chipping away at Rome's boundaries and now controlling land and money that had previously gone to Rome. It became a self-fulfilling cycle of defeat.

All revenue from Britain had vanished, much of Spain was now in barbarian hands, Gaul would not have submitted regular taxes for most of the previous couple of decades. Worst of all, the loss of North Africa – Rome's bread basket – to the Vandals by the end of the 430s was keenly felt. The Vandal leader Geiseric had taken Carthage in 439 and his state remained a Mediterranean superpower until his death in 477. One law of Valentinian III from 451 that aimed at helping African refugees states 'their privilege of the City of Rome shall also be unimpaired until under the auspices of God, it shall come to pass that they return to Africa'.[37] There is a hint of desperate hope in the emperor's words. Numerous other laws around the same time are addressed at maintaining both food infrastructure and defence initiatives, revealing what was at the forefront of people's and the government's minds.

As if that was not bad enough, the remaining parts of the empire were not able to generate revenues as regularly as they had done in the past. After the Goths had left Italy, tax breaks were an inevitable sop to a beleaguered population if Honorius expected to keep any kind of control. But this type of drain on the fisc was no longer sustainable. A series of laws from 440 to 441 attempted to halt pretty much every tax loophole of the Roman economy, right up to the aristocratic landowners themselves.[38]

The unbalanced nature of tax payments is a familiar theme in late antiquity. Salvian of Marseilles writes that the rich are being carried by the poor, who are being strangled by the 'cords of taxation'. Orosius goes even further, complaining that there were Romans who preferred to sustain poverty in freedom among the barbarians than endure the constant oppression of taxation among the Romans. Then as now, carping about unfair taxes is hardly an unfamiliar phenomenon, but here is the other dominant reason why the West failed while the East succeeded. The government in the East had to an extent been colonised by a meritocratic bureaucracy whose success depended on smooth government. In the West the large aristocratic families had annexed government for their own purposes. Put bluntly, the former simply paid more of their taxes than the latter.[39]

There was no way to balance the books. The Roman budget's largest expense throughout late antiquity was the military. As a rule of thumb, defence spending was roughly two-thirds of the budget. The smaller the amount of tax *solidi* in Rome, the smaller the military.

By the 440s, although nominated for consul for an unprecedented third time (this was an honour traditionally reserved for the imperial family) Aetius had to face an entirely new dimension of problems. These sidetracked Aetius from what were, by then, well-developed plans to try to reclaim Africa. They took the form of Attila. He and his Huns were to terrify Rome for the next couple of decades and grind 'almost the whole of Europe to dust'.[40]

As mentioned above, until now the Hun danger to Rome had mostly been second-hand – as the catalyst for other tribes to move into the Roman Empire. It is a fact often conveniently ignored that Rome had made use of the Huns on several occasions in the past. They had been called on to assist the Romans against Alaric and they appear to have helped put down the rebel Emperor Constantine III. The close relationship between Aetius and Attila should not be ignored either. It was Hun troops that had saved Aetius' skin on several occasions, and the two leaders seem to have exchanged both staff and presents.

What changed was the growing power of Attila, ubiquitously described as the scourge of God. Around 440 he and his brother Bleda had started to unify the Huns, swallow up smaller tribes and begun to look across the Danube. This brought the menace to a new level and unleashed a reign of terror across the Continent that would be halted only by Attila's death.

The 50-year-old king (he was born around 383) could now make his ambitions felt. Throughout the 440s he ransacked the Balkans three times, bringing down numerous cities; Nis for example in 442. After each attack, Attila was bought off by the Eastern empire. In around 420, Attila's uncle had negotiated an annual tribute of 350lb of gold from Byzantium, which was doubled by the time Attila himself came to power. By 443 the emperor had agreed to make a back payment of 6,000lb of gold to the Huns.

The lack of Hun finds is noticeable. This missing archaeological footprint is partly down to a nomadic culture and a comparatively short period of domination, but it is possible nevertheless to get a sense of their wealth. A dig in the Hungarian town of Pannonhalma in 1979 revealed a grave of incredible riches: swords, horse bits, jewellery and, of course, decorations for the Hun recurved bow, the secret weapon that allowed them a speed and density of fire that, as John Man, recent biographer of Attila writes, would not be seen again 'until the invention of repeating guns in the latter part of the nineteenth century'.[41]

By the middle of the decade Attila had had his brother murdered and took over as sole warlord. He was now unstoppable. The Hun leader was a monarch, surrounded by a coterie of lieutenants whom he kept close and whose loyalty seems to have been absolute. There was nothing the Roman army could do. It could not cope with the Hun cavalry and their archers. More significantly, service for Rome had brought the Huns some skill in siege warfare, which struck at the heart of Roman civilisation.

By 447 it was time to sue for peace. There is no mistaking the punitive and humiliating terms the Romans were forced to sign – not even their politicians could put a positive complexion on them. Nothing better captures the contempt that Attila had for the imperial throne than the story of the Hun king's behaviour after he had captured Milan. In one of the palaces he saw a picture of Roman emperors sitting on golden thrones, with dead barbarians scattered at their feet. Attila found the painter and ordered him to paint himself on a throne, while Roman emperors poured gold out of sacks at his feet. It does not matter whether it was true or not; it does matter that it was believed.[42]

A contemporary called Priscus – we shall meet him at length in the following chapter – describes the conditions of the treaty:

The terms were as follows: that fugitives should be handed over to the Huns and 6,000lb gold be paid to complete the outstanding instalments of tribute; that the tribute be set at 2,100lb gold a year from now on; that 12 gold pieces be paid for each Roman prisoner of war who escaped and reached his home territory without ransom, and if those who received him did not pay, they were to hand over the fugitive; and that the Romans were to receive no barbarian who fled to them.[43]

It was obvious who now called the shots.

TWO

Breaking Up is Hard to Do

In early 449 one of Attila's most trusted lieutenants, a Hun by the name of Edeco, arrived in Constantinople to negotiate with Emperor Theodosius II. Attila was demanding a significant area of land south of the River Danube, roughly from what is Serbia's capital Belgrade across into Bulgaria and five days' journey deep, which he claimed was his as a result of the treaty he had secured two years previously. This was on top of the asylum seekers who had still not been returned.

Accompanying Edeco, seemingly his deputy, though he saw himself as an equal, was a Roman called Orestes, a charismatic, good-looking and clearly talented young man, 'A man of the greatest discretion,' writes Procopius.[1] It is one of those odd, slightly incongruous facts of history, like knowing that Mahatma Gandhi was a stretcher-bearer in South Africa during the Boer War that sticks in your mind. This Orestes was the last of Rome's great kingmakers and father of Romulus Augustulus, Rome's last emperor.

His date of birth is not recorded, but it must have been some time before 430. His own youth had been buffeted by European politics. The son of the diplomat Tatulus, from whose name we can gather little other than a non-Roman heritage, Orestes was born into a wealthy Pannonian Roman family from near the River Save. On what was effectively the northern boundary to the Balkans, the area had found itself subject to Attila after one of Rome's earlier treaties with the Huns. Either feeling neglected by Rome or weighing which side offered the best prospects for promotion, Orestes entered Hun service. He clearly proved competent. When we meet him he held the position of *notarius*. This is often still translated as 'secretary', though what must have been an incredibly demanding and exposed position should carry the idea of chief of staff rather than that of scribe or personal assistant.

That Edeco, Orestes' superior on the trip, was the father of Odovacer, the barbarian who was to supplant Romulus, remains a deep historical irony and adds, as many have noted, a touch of dramatic completeness to the era.

When Attila's envoys arrived in Constantinople they immediately went on the offensive. The Romans, claimed Edeco, had reneged on the terms of the previous treaty. They had neither withdrawn from territory south of the Danube, nor had they returned the Hun refugees. The choice was simple: submit or suffer the consequences. Some idea of Attila's power can be gleaned from his demand that the emperor send diplomats – not foreign office flunkies, but consular-level senior officials – to a summit meeting in his capital.

Edeco left and was brought to another part of the palace for a further meeting. There he met the power behind the throne, the greedy and unpleasant eunuch Chrysaphius Zstommas. It soon became apparent that Chrysaphius had a hidden agenda, a proposed assassination attempt that brings to mind many of the CIA's inept bids in more recent times to remove the Cuban dictator Fidel Castro.

As Edeco made politely flattering noises about the palace, Chrysaphius crudely suggested that the Hun too could own such a big house if he started to work for the Romans. Again politely, Edeco responded that it would be inappropriate to work for someone else without getting Attila's permission first. After more probing by Chrysaphius about Edeco's precise relationship to

Attila, so transparent that it is impossible to believe that Edeco did not see through it, the eunuch invited Edeco to supper, though without Orestes or the other diplomats.

After extracting promises of non-disclosure, Chrysaphius made his pitch at dinner. If Edeco were to return to the barbarian court, murder Attila and return to Byzantium, he could live the rest of his life in luxury. Edeco played along and demanded money, some 50lb of gold, to bribe his own men to help. Chrysaphius offered to give it to him there and then, but Edeco demurred. Attila, he said, was suspicious of embassies. He monitored all gifts carefully and this sum of gold would be hard to hide from his colleagues. Instead, he suggested, the interpreter Vigilas should be sent with him while he reported back on the news of the prisoners in Roman captivity. Only then would Edeco tell Byzantium via Vigilas how he wanted his cash.

A refined plan was now put into action. To distract attention from Vigilas, a diplomat named Maximinus became the fall guy in the plot.[2] He was something of a Byzantine trouble-shooter who had also been a member of a commission in the 430s to write a compilation of Roman law, called the Theodosian Code. Since he knew nothing of Chrysaphius' plans he was the perfect choice to head up a fake mission to Attila to discuss the issues that the Hun had raised.

We are fortunate that a highly detailed account of this mission has survived. One of those travelling with Maximinus was his friend Priscus of Panium, a slightly fussy bureaucrat who came along as a friend rather than in any official capacity, and who wrote down a travelogue of the embassy.

Accompanied therefore by the Hun contingent led by Edeco and Orestes, Maximinus, Priscus, Vigilas and a Hun-speaking Roman who had business to conduct with another of Attila's Roman secretaries, set out from Byzantium. Two weeks' travelling brought them to Sofia. Cross-cultural conviviality seemed appropriate that evening, so the Romans invited the barbarians to dinner. Toasts were raised until Vigilas, who appears to have become more than a little tipsy, injected a sour note that almost triggered a fully blown diplomatic incident. After the Hun contingent had toasted Attila and the Romans had raised their cups to Theodosius, Vigilas mentioned that it was unfair to compare a god and a man. It took all Maximinus' persuasion to calm down the Huns, and he ended the evening by flattering both Orestes and Edeco, giving them silk cloth and pearls as gifts.

An already strange situation took a further turn for the bizarre the next day. Orestes went out of his way to comment on the gifts. He said that it was wise of Maximinus to avoid giving offence, unlike the Byzantine court. There, he complained, Edeco had been taken off to dinner without him. Maximinus and Priscus were confused at the outburst, concerned enough to mention it to Vigilas, who told them it was nothing to worry about. Orestes was, after all, only a servant and secretary to the great Attila, while Edeco was a great warrior and clearly the Roman's superior.

Vigilas' excuse was just that – an attempt to distract Maximinus and Priscus. Nonetheless it is a curious action on the part of Orestes. What was he trying to do? Was he genuinely resentful that he and Edeco had been treated differently? Was he trying to indicate that he too wished to be bribed? Did he think that Maximinus was in on the plot and was letting him know that he knew? Was he simply warning the Romans that Edeco could not be trusted? The incident raises many more questions than it answers.

This strange party soon reached Nis, a once-important imperial centre. The former home town of Constantine the Great had been destroyed by war and disease six years previously. There had been little sign of any attempt at reconstruction. 'The river banks were full of the bones of those killed in war,' writes Priscus. The embassy continued in increasingly disastrous fashion. If Orestes' outburst had been perplexing, it was nothing compared to what now met the embassy when it reached one of Attila's camps. A party of Huns, including Orestes, appeared before the Romans, asking them what they wanted to talk to Attila about.

It was a particularly nasty form of psychological torture. It was apparent that Attila already knew not only everything that had happened in Byzantium between Edeco and Chrysaphius, but even the emperor's instructions to the diplomats. Maximinus must have realised that there was an agenda to which he was not privy. It is to his credit that he refused to turn tail, insisting that he talk to Attila in person. His persistence paid off. Although diplomatic niceties with the Hun leader's deputies continued for several days, they eventually got to meet Attila in person.

It is a significant moment in history. Priscus gives us history's first eyewitness description of Attila, and it is worth citing in full:

He was a man born into the world to shake the nations, the scourge of all lands, who in some way terrified all mankind with the dreadful rumours spoken about him. He walked in an arrogant manner, rolling his eyes this way and that, so that the strength of his proud spirit showed in his body's movement. It is true that he loved war and yet he was restrained in action, mighty in counsel, gracious to petitioners and lenient to those who were once received into his protection. He was short, with a broad chest and a large head: his eyes were small, his beard thin and sprinkled with grey. He had a flat nose and dark features, showing the evidence of his origin.[3]

But the meeting ended in an impasse. While Maximinus and Priscus were still not aware of what was going on around them, Edeco sprung the trap on the hapless interpreter. He now told the inept Vigilas to head back to Constantinople to get the money, his 50lb of gold. Maximinus and Priscus remained effectively stranded, part of Attila's entourage, reduced to following him round his empire before ending up in one of his permanent palace compounds.

There they briefly met up with a set of Western diplomats in a similar position to themselves. They were attempting to smooth matters over with the Hun king on behalf of Emperor Valentinian III, or more accurately with Aetius. These envoys are worth pausing over because the members of this delegation included both of Romulus Augustulus' grandfathers – Orestes' own father Tatulus, who was visiting his son, and Romulus, Orestes' father-in-law, after whom the future emperor would be named. In the account Romulus comes across as a clued-up man. 'An ambassador of long experience', is Priscus' description, and he exhibits both a familiarity with Attila (he gives the Eastern envoys tips on etiquette) but also a general knowledge of the East.[4] The fact that they were visiting Orestes was no coincidence, but a sign of how well placed he now was within Attila's inner circle and that this had been recognised in Rome.

For the Eastern legation itself it meant several weeks of limbo. Nothing long term was achieved, and little of short-term value either (although they managed to negotiate the release of a Roman lady and her children). Perhaps the best that can be said for it is that Maximinus and Priscus survived with their heads still on their shoulders.

As for Vigilas, he was captured as soon as his feet touched Hun soil and he was made to confess all. Fortunately for him, the worst that happened was that he was made to ransom his son, who had travelled with him, for another 50lb of gold. It is hard to disagree with Peter Heather who sees this magnanimity as deliberate. Rather than killing all the Roman diplomats, who had, after all, broken all the unspoken rules that protected them, Attila 'saw the plot as another opportunity to reinforce his psychological domination over the east Romans'.[5]

Orestes was ordered back to Constantinople with another of Attila's lieutenants. It was a canny and symbolic choice on Attila's part. He had picked a Roman and his uncle's old number two – a reminder to Constantinople both that Romans worked for him and of the longevity of Hun power so far. There, in front of the 41-year-old emperor, Orestes appeared with a bag of gold around his neck – the bag that Vigilas had filled with money for Edeco. Orestes asked the emperor and Chrysaphius whether they recognised it. As he did so, his colleague had been ordered to say that although both Theodosius and Attila were noble-born, only Attila still lived up to his heritage. It was a dramatic moment.

It is an incident too that must have had powerful effect on Orestes. The impact for a young man, seeing the emperor shown up as a duplicitous buffoon, watching as his first minister Chrysaphius tried not to squirm, must have been an unpleasant revelation. To read into this event Orestes' suspicion of imperial power or to suggest that the showdown in Constantinople planted the seeds for his future revolt is going too far, but at the very least it was an apprenticeship for him in understanding the source of true power and authority.

At the start of 451 Attila and the Huns started westwards. Their approach into France was watched with horror. Half a million men, writes Jordanes, was the size of Attila's army, a reflection less of actual troop numbers than their impact. Sidonius Apollinaris remembered how his force 'poured into the whole north of Gaul'. Attila intended to wipe out the Western armies and take Rome. There is the story that he sent an ambassador to Emperor Valentinian in Rome, asking the emperor to prepare the palace for him to move in as he was already crossing the Rhine.[6] One gets the feeling that this was more than just bravado.

The odds were not in Aetius' favour. Attila had already taken Belgium by the time that Aetius crossed the Alps with his 'thin meagre force of auxiliaries'. He did not have any legionaries with him and his chances of recruiting en route were slim given the famine that was ravaging Italy at the time. When Aetius linked up with his reluctant ally, the king of the Visigoths, at the end of April, he was heading up a distinctly mongrel army. Jordanes lists them as 'Franks, Sarmatians, Armoricians, Liticians, Burgundians, Saxons, Riparians, Olibriones . . . and some other Celtic or German tribes'.[7] It was hardly a coherent fighting force.

In June Attila attacked, but was unable to take Orleans: his assault was beaten off. 'Attacked and breached, but never plundered', is the contemporary conclusion.[8]

A week later it came to battle, the Huns versus the once-mighty Roman military machine. It was the last great field battle of the Western Roman army. Like Charles Martel's successful repelling of the Moors at the battle of Poitiers in October 732 or Jan Sobieski's protection of Vienna from the Ottoman army in September 1683, the battle of the Catalaunian Plains (sometimes called the battle of Chalôns) saved European culture. Aetius' successful defence against the Huns is a defining moment in Europe history. Yet for as significant a conflict as this it is a surprise how little we know about it. Even the date is uncertain, though 20 June is usually given.

Details are vague. We do not even know for sure where it took place. It was, writes Jordanes, fierce, confused, monstrous and unrelenting, 'a fight whose like no ancient time has ever recorded'.[9] He may be right, but it was by no means decisive. In the end Aetius' ally, the Visigothic king, was killed and Attila was allowed to withdraw. The Hun leader may have been knocked back but he was by no means defeated. That the conflict had been a draw can be inferred from Attila's raid on Illyria that September. The following summer, he raided Italy.

The low point of that campaign was the siege of Aquileia in 452. It was a long entrenchment on both sides, though the city eventually fell. At dawn one day, so the story went, Attila saw a stork leaving the city with its young. It is an image that was much used by medieval scribes and appears in numerous manuscripts. The Hun took this avian departure as a sign that he was going to take the city. He did and 'so cruelly devastated it as scarcely to leave a trace to be seen'.[10] The city is best known for its archaeological remains around the port on the River Natissa. But a sense of this period is given by incredible mosaics, the rivals of anything else in the empire, in the Crypt of Excavations in the Patriarchal basilica where foundations can also be seen of the original structure that was destroyed by Attila.

After Aquileia, Milan and Pavia soon fell too. It must indeed have felt as if he had 'demolished almost the whole of Italy'. But Attila did not approach Rome. At the time no one knew why. It is said that he was scared of bad luck; that he had been warned that when Alaric had done so he had died soon afterwards. In an encounter famously preserved in legend and art, Attila was met on the banks of the River Mincio in Lombardy by a delegation led by Pope Leo the Great, who persuaded him to leave Italy. Unsurprisingly, that is the version promoted by the Church. Rather more plausibly, Attila himself seems to have decided to withdraw. The effects of the Italian famine could not have been eased at all by marauding Huns, which can have done nothing to make the commander's logistics any easier. Indeed, one chronicler states bluntly that the Huns were victims of famine and disease.[11]

Attila did withdraw but was never to attack anywhere ever again. In 453, on the night of his wedding to his latest beautiful wife, Ildico, Attila drank heavily. Asleep on his back, he suffered a nosebleed and suffocated. It was a death more typical of rock nobility than the man who had terrified Europe, but one should also remember that he was almost seventy.[12]

He was buried with treasures and weapons taken from his enemies in a coffin bound with gold, silver and finally iron. Those who had dug the barrow were killed and interred with him so that no robbers would ever disturb his rest and Attila was left to make his way into the afterlife and European legend. Without its head, the Hun Empire began to disintegrate rapidly. Its physical presence vanished as quickly as it had arrived. In less than two decades after Attila's death it went from superpower to nothing.

The death of the Hun signalled an unravelling within Europe. We know that Orestes was with Attila in Italy, but after this we lose sight of him for the next twenty years.[13] He vanishes into the historical whirlpool of the collapse of the Hun Empire that tugged the Roman Empire down with it.

The splinter regimes of unwilling Hun vassals did as much to hasten the end of the empire as the Hun hordes had done, with the result that the rest of Valentinian III's reign was a disaster. An Italy now exhausted by famine, disease and the Huns remained unable to recapture the crucial grainfields of North Africa from the Vandals. With no common enemy to unite them, there was much squabbling between the 28-year-old Valentinian and Aetius. Two events brought matters to a head. On the death of Theodosius II in Constantinople in July 450 after a riding accident, Valentinian considered making a bid for the Eastern throne and unifying the empire. Aetius quite reasonably, though unpopularly, advised the imperial popinjay against it. The second event was Aetius' all-too transparent manoeuvring to make himself the next emperor by putting his son forward as a husband for one of the emperor's two daughters.

Resentment spilled over in the emperor, who was hardly the most mature of characters at the best of times. (It is hard to disagree with one ancient writer's description of him as a 'mad eunuch' and a more modern view of him as a 'selfish and indolent voluptuary'.[14]) He had been dominated by his mother until he was 18 and by Aetius pretty much ever since. Now that Attila was dead, the general's use was pretty much at an end. The emperor's solution was to have the general killed: in a meeting of the imperial finance committee at the end of September 454, the emperor himself and the head of his household stabbed Aetius to death.

Valentinian was not to survive this betrayal long. It was generally believed at the time that the emperor had cut off his right hand with his left. The vultures began to circle, and within six months two guards, who had been close to Aetius, killed him on the Campus Martius in Rome.[15]

The subsequent twenty years are a confused period of virtually unremitting disaster as the remains of the Roman Empire suffered under the emperors who ruled after the death of Valentinian III. Little wonder that the chronicler Count Marcellinus dated the collapse of Roman sovereignty from the murder of Aetius: 'With him fell the western Kingdom and it has not as yet been able to be restored.'[16] The eight men who reigned from March 455 to August 475 have become known as the shadow emperors, some ruling only a few months, and even contemporaries had little to say about them. 'Although I know their names well, I won't mention them at all,' writes Procopius. 'They only lived a short time after attaining the office and as a result accomplished nothing worth mentioning.'[17]

The ringleader in Valentinian's, and indeed Aetius' murder, Petronius Maximus, was crowned emperor straight away, but lasted a mere couple of months before being torn limb from limb by a Roman mob while trying to escape a Vandal attack on Rome in June. His successor Avitus (coincidentally Sidonius Apollinaris' father-in-law) soon fell too. He had been unable to achieve any kind of popularity in the face of the Vandal sack of Rome, was guilty of too close a relationship with the Goths, failed to solve the financial crisis and had managed to alienate the senate, the people and the military.

The real power from 456 to 472 was Flavius Ricimer, the barbarian general and military dictator who made and broke emperors. He dominated what was left of Europe much more so than either of his predecessors, Stilicho or Aetius. They had at least worked with just one emperor. Ricimer developed such a power base on his own that one of the chroniclers even refers to him as King Ricimer.[18]

Like his patrician predecessors, Ricimer is a confusing character and a much debated one. There are certain characters in the classical world who have been politicised out of all proportion to their actual impact, the slave revolutionary Spartacus and the Cheruscan leader Arminius to name just two examples. Ricimer is another. Many historians portray him as essentially evil or at least barbarian through and through, which amounts to pretty much the same thing. The reality is much more complex. Ricimer does seem to have been motivated by self-interest. But his power came from the Roman Empire, so he had no interest in seeing that harmed, and he did provide a limited continuity that had been missing.

He was a noble barbarian, linked to three Germanic royal families, though identified most closely with that of his mother, who was a daughter of a king of the Visigoths. Born in the 420s, by the time he came to power as a commander-in-chief and kingmaker in 456 he was in his late 20s or early 30s.

It is not known how he managed to achieve as much power as he did, though he was one of Aetius' officers and possibly had a personal connection to the inner circle through Aetius' wife, who was also of royal Gothic blood. It is also unclear how he managed to maintain the loyalty of the army throughout his career – through personal charm rather than his aristocratic heritage seems likely.

By the time that Avitus had been deposed in October 456 (the sexagenarian was made bishop of Placentia but died soon afterwards, possibly poisoned) Ricimer was senior military commander and already plotting to put his friend Majorian on the throne. The two were a revolutionary dream team; Ricimer, the most influential general in the empire, Majorian a charismatic leader with the support of Aetius' army.

Most of 457 was an interregnum, since Majorian was not formally installed until 28 December in Ravenna. But Ricimer was made patrician at the end of February, with apparently no authority other than the army. This is a significant step, as this is the first time that we see someone with official power who does not owe it to the ruler in the West. It is a subtle but important shift. Both Stilicho and Aetius paid at least lip service to the idea that they were subservient to an emperor.

It soon became clear quite how much influence Ricimer had. The first law passed by the emperor on 11 January 458 says that 'The watchful care of military matters will be Our concern, as well as the concern of . . . Ricimer'.[19] The constitutional implications of the phrase have been disproportionately parsed. But what is clear is that although Majorian had qualities, Ricimer had the real power. The major difference between his rule and that of Romulus' father is that as a barbarian and as an Arian Ricimer could never have been a contender on his own. In sharp contrast, when the time came for Orestes' coup, he benefited both from being a Roman and from having a precedent to follow.

The biggest issue of the day was the defence of Italy in the light of the Vandal assault. That threat from Africa dominated many of the moves for the next decade or so. But behind the scenes, Ricimer wanted power for himself. While Majorian was out of Italy and distracted by what turned out to be an abortive assault on North Africa, Ricimer plotted against him. When the emperor returned, Ricimer was prepared to take power. At the start of August 461, he had Majorian stripped, beaten and decapitated in the north Italian town of Tortona. Why did he bother to revolt? He had the power anyway. All kinds of ingenious theories have been proposed. That the emperor had become a hindrance is just one of the more popular suggestions. The main one, however, appears to be just that Majorian existed.

By mid-November Ricimer had picked a more pliable puppet called Libius Severus. He had been chosen because such a recommendation would cause no problems with the senate and because Severus had no military experience whatsoever and would not get under the patrician's feet. The gap between emperor and patrician began to widen. Diplomats were sent to North Africa in Ricimer's own name, rather than that of the emperor. If voices were raised in concern, they were silenced by the fact that he successfully warded off an attack on northern Italy. Certainly the archaeological evidence that can be generally dated to this period confirms Ricimer's growing power. His name, for example, starts to appear on coins – monograms including the letters R, C, M and E. Although there remains some debate as to precisely when they were minted, it does not really matter whether it was during an interregnum or an emperor's reign: it was a major step.

Severus was to die on 14 November 465, maybe and not implausibly poisoned, fated to be forgotten by all. Little is remembered or worth remembering from his four-year reign, with one notable exception. Possibly in 463, probably at some point in his reign, Romulus Augustulus was born. No contemporary historian thought his birth important enough to record, but in the Roman world a boy became a man at the age of 14. The description of Romulus as a boy in 477 gives us a broad timeframe for his birth.[20]

Orestes either left Hun service after the Italian campaigns or found his way back to Italy soon afterwards in the confusion and factional splintering after the death of Attila. Given that both his father and his father-in-law, as diplomats, were trusted Aetian loyalists, it would not be out of the question that he aimed for Roman territory.

Although Orestes had been by no means a prisoner, some slight sense of how unsettling a time this must have been, with refugees pouring back into the empire, can be seen in a letter that Pope Leo wrote to the bishop of Aquileia in 458 discussing the return of Romans from the Huns, presumably captured by Attila six years previously. The pope is writing specifically to address the problem of women who had remarried while their husbands were in captivity, and his mention of 'the wounds which have been inflicted by the attacks of the enemy', give some insight into the chaos.[21]

But after Aetius' murder and the Vandal danger in Italy had subsided, Orestes seems to have moved in the direction of Noricum, Dalmatia and Pannonia. He had been married to Romulus' daughter Barbaria since the end of the 440s and it is known that her family had been rooted in northern Italy, Noricum, Dalmatia and Pannonia since the first century. The family's origins were in manufacturing (they appear to have made tiles), and by the second century they could boast both a consul and an emperor's wife, even if the marriage had been a brief one.

It is guesswork, but it seems likely that Orestes ended up, at least for a time, in Passau, one of the last Roman strongholds in the Roman province of Noricum. Certainly that is where Tatulus and Romulus the Elder's mission to Attila had started, and both Orestes and Barbaria had close ties to the region.[22]

There is a rather confused passage that adds another dimension to Romulus and his family. It might answer the question of why it was that Barbaria would have been comparatively old for the period – at the youngest in her late 20s – when Romulus was born. One sixth-century chronicler refers to a son of Orestes called Herculanus. It has been suggested that this was Romulus' name at birth. It was certainly not uncommon for an emperor to take a new name when he ascended the throne, as Octavian did when he became Augustus. But that seems unlikely given that

Romulus' maternal grandfather was also called Romulus. If the name is not simply scribal error, then Herculanus might have been an elder brother – the obligatory heir, while Romulus was the spare. An unfortunate accident or illness could easily have accounted for his younger brother taking the throne.[23]

Back in Rome, Severus' successor after a lengthy hiatus (until April 467) was the Emperor Anthemius. For those almost eighteen months, Ricimer was sole ruler, and it is a sign of his desire to placate the East that he now accepted an appointment from the Eastern emperor in Constantinople. The disastrous reign of this Greek, however, highlights how far apart Rome and Byzantium had drifted. Even though the empire had been unified centuries before and Greek was, after Latin, its second language, the fact that Anthemius was a Greek-speaker was beyond the pale to Rome. One Western writer called him *graeculus*. Literally meaning 'little Greek' or 'Greekling' as it is still given in older dictionaries, the implication was 'bloody foreigner'. It was the same xenophobic term of abuse used a century earlier about the Emperor Julian by his mutinous troops in Gaul. It made the distinct difference between us and them, and was a dry run for the commonplace bigotry of later years towards the Byzantine Empire based on accusations that it was not remotely Roman and entirely Greek.[24]

Although his reign had started well, and he himself came from good stock (he could claim descent from the house of Constantine, which would have had some cachet), Anthemius managed to alienate Ricimer, annoy the pope, and lose credibility by failing to stem the tide of barbarian incursions. His language and ethnicity was now something to mock.

Ricimer's glamorous marriage to Anthemius' daughter (Sidonius Apollinaris who happened to be in Rome wrote that 'the wealth of both empires was blown to the winds in the process') is the clearest sign, if any doubt remained, of his intention to consolidate his power and was clearly one of the conditions of accepting the Eastern nomination. Here again it is possible to see how Orestes' power echoed but subtly differed from Ricimer's. As a Roman, marriage for recognition's sake was a hoop through which he would never have to jump.[25]

The greater surprise is that Ricimer and Anthemius somehow managed to work together for three years before they came to open conflict in 470. The shot across the bows was when the emperor had one of Ricimer's supporters executed. The conflict soon degenerated into civil war, and Ricimer blockaded Rome.

When Olybrius was appointed emperor in April 472, his coronation was marked by double-crossing, diplomatic legerdemain and, as so often at this time, set against a background of civil war. Few doubt that Olybrius (originally sent by Emperor Leo in the East to arbitrate between the two sides) had been named emperor before the death of Anthemius. Ricimer was already in revolt when Olybrius appeared in Rome and had, to all intents and purposes, isolated the emperor in the imperial palace in Rome since March. Guards had been placed at the port and other points of entry into Italy, and no one was allowed in or out without Ricimer's say-so.

By the summer, the effects of the siege were being felt and there are indications of soldiers gradually changing sides. As for Anthemius, he was killed on 11 July. The most common tradition has it that he was killed in the church of St Peter's in Rome by Ricimer's nephew and deputy, Gundobad, though another version suggests that the emperor had tried to escape the city dressed as a monk and was beheaded in what is now the Basilica of Santa Maria in Trastevere.

Of all the so-called shadow emperors, Olybrius had the shortest reign, a mere seven months, though ironically he had been a good choice for emperor. From the Roman senate's point of view he was an aristocrat, patrician and former consul. The inherent conservatism of that body should never be underestimated. It was just as important to them that he was not a Greek. From Ricimer's point of view Olybrius was commended by his age – we can presume that he was at least in his 50s – and from what little may be inferred from his coins (they are overtly Christian, encouraging the 'salvation of the republic' and the 'salvation of the world') was more interested in his soul than in power. That kind of a man was unlikely to have too many ideas of his own about governance.

But Ricimer was about to lose the one battle he could never predict or win. He was soon to fall ill and die, in a month, in fact, after 'vomiting a great deal of blood'.[26] Dates are vague – some say 18 or 19 August – and his nephew Gundobad slipped into his position as commander-in-chief. By the end of October, or at the latest the beginning of November, Olybrius himself had died of unspecified swelling.

Uncertainty now reigned until the following March, though as commander-in-chief, Gundobad was de facto ruler, especially as he had the weight of the army behind him. There were few who would have been prepared to go up against Ricimer's nephew and it is likely that Ricimer formally appointed him his successor on his deathbed. Then, in March, Glycerius was eventually crowned in Ravenna, as one chronicler has it 'more by presumption than by election'. He was a military man, a senior officer in the imperial guard and presumably he fitted the bill. It can be taken for granted that he had been one of Ricimer's supporters. Little is known about his reign and less can be guessed, though the comments about him in the chronicles are generally positive. One writer from the north of Italy, where he remained for most of his reign, refers to 'the numerous things he did for the well-being of many people'. This seems to refer to the diplomatic success that Glycerius had in diverting a Visigothic invasion and palming the threat off on to Gaul instead.[27]

Although by no means an official emperor in the sense that he had been approved by Byzantium, he, or rather Gundobad, appears to have gone out of his way to appease the East. There was no consul nominated, for example, for the year AD 474. Despite this obvious attempt to defer to Byzantium, moves had already been made against Glycerius. The Emperor Leo, nicknamed 'the butcher', had nominated Julius Nepos, a relation by marriage to the throne (he was the husband of his wife's niece), and scion of the virtually hereditary rulers of Dalmatia, to lead the campaign and then take the throne.

Plans were delayed at the start of the year because of the death of the 73-year-old Emperor Leo of dysentery in January 474. He was succeeded by his next direct male descendant, his grandson, the 7-year-old Leo II. The boy's father Zeno, Leo the Elder's son-in-law, acted as regent. But this was to signal no change in imperial policy or reprieve for the West.

As soon as Julius Nepos appeared at Portus, Rome's port on the right bank at the mouth of the River Tiber, in late June, the Emperor Glycerius surrendered without a fight, without a blow being struck. Initially he seems to have had every intention of resistance, but the disappearance of Gundobad, who returned to Gaul to become king of the Burgundians on the death of his father, seems to have taken the fight out of him. It is possible that Glycerius had misunderstood the strength of his power base. At any rate he was pardoned by the new emperor, or at least spared, and appointed bishop of Split. The shift into the Church was to have a precedent for Romulus Augustulus a few years later.

Leo II had died of natural causes through a childhood illness by mid-November and was succeeded by his father. With Zeno on the throne in the East and Julius Nepos in the West, a curious calm, the eye of a storm, now descended on the Western empire for his fourteen months as emperor. It was certainly the last time that two emperors ruled jointly. Out of Ravenna, the new Western emperor appears to have injected a verve and zest into the ever-tiring empire. There was a fleeting spirit of hope and togetherness. Coins, for example, were issued in the name of the emperor of the East, emphasising the close connections between the two rulers. Indeed, gold *solidi* were struck in both Leo's and Zeno's names.

This enthusiasm and spirit of cooperation did not last long in the face of external pressures. The Mediterranean became increasingly dangerous as pirates dominated the sea and parts of Africa fell to the Vandals. Ignoring that which he did not have the resources to fix, Nepos seems to have devoted a considerable amount of time and effort to secure what was left of imperial Gaul.

Over the past five years imperial Gaul had not so much collapsed as sagged under constant Gothic pressure. In 469 Euric, the king of the Visigoths, successfully launched a series of attacks on several fronts to create a unified Gothic nation. He was to be remarkably successful both as a politician and as a general. At his death in 484, his kingdom encompassed most of the Iberian peninsula and two-thirds of France. The king, probably in his early to mid-50s, attacked the Bretons across the River Loire and pushed into the Auvergne and down as far as Spain. But he was also being pressed. The presence of the Franks on his northern border was a danger to his kingdom, as was that of the Burgundians, who were based around Lyons; and none of this was made any easier to deal with given the number of bandits preying on citizens.

It became clear to Euric that the way to contain these dangers was to attack the city of Clermont in the Auvergne. That would give him enough resources to resist the Franks and checkmate the Burgundians at the same time. The Romans in the city were as aware of this as the Visigoths. They had sent an embassy to Rome for help two years earlier, in 467. The news for the Auvergne was not good. Sidonius Apollinaris' note a few years later is gloomy.

'Our people are at the last gasp; freedom is almost dead,' he writes.[28] Rome, he continues, is powerless and the emperor has no resources. An army was sent from Italy in 471, but it was decisively beaten near Arles. There was no question of another. The following year, succession issues and the fight between Ricimer and Anthemius meant that no resources could be spared.

For three years, from 471 to 474, Clermont was raided every year by the Visigoths. From within the city, Sidonius Apollinaris' letters are clearly exaggerations, but the descriptions of the half-ruined walls, flame-scorched buildings, bones of unburied dead, the famine and the strain on the people's faces speak for themselves.[29]

The Clermont resistance, such as it was within the city, was organised by Ecdicius, Sidonius' brother-in-law, son of the Emperor Avitus and an imperial general. Sidonius wrote him a stirring letter describing his arrival. 'At midday, and right across the middle of the plain, you brought your little company of eighteen men safe through some thousands of the Goths, a feat which posterity will surely deem incredible.'[30] Ecdicius then raised an army out of his own pocket to lead the city's defence. The heroic language cannot disguise how inadequate the force was that was to save the city or how empty the imperial treasury must have been if individuals had to raise armies themselves.

There was always a division in Roman society between Rome the concept and Rome the reality. At the end of the fourth century the poet Ausonius of Bordeaux captured this idea of what has been dubbed dual citizenship when he wrote: 'This is my own country; but Rome stands above all countries. I love Bordeaux, I venerate Rome.'[31]

But as Jill Harries points out in her essential study of the period, with the accession to the throne of Julius Nepos, this division now deepened. On one hand Sidonius Apollinaris could call him 'a true Emperor in character no less than prowess'. Yet on the other, in a letter to a relative who was being accused of being an agitator for the new emperor, he could refer to a whispering campaign of 'malicious charges' from 'venomous tongues'. This was hardly the tone of an imperial loyalist, but the town of Vaison, where his relative lived, was solidly in Burgundian hands. Better to collaborate than die. Those like Sidonius had to reconcile their ingrained love of and loyalty to Rome with the awareness that it was an impotent mirage. This again is a crucial point about the decline of the West. People will cling on to an idea, nurture it and celebrate it, but can quite happily collaborate if it means putting food on the table and staying alive.[32]

Julius Nepos did attempt a diplomatic solution with Euric. In the spring of 475 the experienced ecclesiastical diplomat Bishop Epiphanius of Pavia was sent to Toulouse to broker a deal, and was followed by four local bishops who hammered out the terms of the deal. In fact Epiphanius had nothing with which to negotiate. The bishop's biographer (presumably the information comes from the bishop himself) admits that Nepos wanted to defend by diplomacy what he could not protect by force. The news soon filtered out that the price of keeping Provence within the empire was the Auvergne. Bitterly Sidonius Apollinaris writes: 'our enslavement was made the price of security for a third party'.[33]

That summer, Ecdicius, Julius Nepos' commander-in-chief, was removed from office under somewhat hazy circumstances. It is difficult to work out exactly what was happening. It is possible that the emperor simply needed him, both his physical and moral presence, in Italy, but then again there is also a chance that the general already knew that Clermont and the Auvergne were to be sacrificed. Unable to help in any way, he did not want to be the one to hand over the keys.

Ecdicius' replacement was Orestes. His rapid promotion under Julius Nepos would suggest that Orestes had indeed gone to Dalmatia and taken service under the current emperor rather than having kicked his heels around Ricimer's Rome. This idea is given additional credence by the connection his wife and her family had with the region. At any rate, Orestes had no personal attachments in Gaul and his years of experience in Attila's service had made him comfortable in dealing with barbarians, which made him an ideal choice for the emperor. Nonetheless, by the end of the summer Orestes had repaid his promotion by leading a revolt.

As a consequence, Romulus Augustulus and his immediate relatives would become the first family of the Western empire for a brief eighteen months.

Nothing is known of the circumstances of Orestes' revolt other than that he had the opportunity and was in charge of a significant number of troops, presumably from garrisons in the north. This northern support base is backed up by one northern writer's positive description of him (he calls Orestes by his title of 'patrician', in stark contrast to the wicked heart and ambition of his opponent) and corroborated by the fact that the best coins of Romulus' reign were minted in Milan. If one were to hazard a guess, irregular payment must have been either the spark for his revolutionary fire or the excuse for it which was then fanned by resentment at selling out the Auvergne.[34]

One chronicler seems to suggest that the signs of Orestes' revolutionary tendencies were apparent from the beginning – 'the spur of vanity prevented Julius Nepos from prudently anticipating the causes of his own deposition' – but this was written after the fact. As one modern historian so succinctly puts it: 'With his unique combination of qualities, he was doubtless able to attract the support of various elements in Italy who were dissatisfied equally with domination by a barbarian generalissimo and domination by an emperor imposed by the East.' By the end of

August, Orestes had taken Ravenna, and with remarkably little effort.[35]

It is hard to see how Orestes could have been better placed to achieve support. He was not a barbarian like Ricimer and had not been foisted on Italy from Constantinople. He seems to have had the weight of the army behind him – supported undoubtedly by his brother, Romulus' uncle, Paul, who was a senior figure in the regime – and Nepos made no attempt at a resistance. It is difficult to see how he might have done so. He had been emperor for such a brief time and it is unlikely that he had managed yet to create his own support base in Italy. And if Orestes had indeed been promoted from Nepos' inner circle, it speaks volumes about their loyalty. Much better to regroup and ask Constantinople for help. In what one chronicle calls 'such desperate conditions', Nepos fled across the Adriatic Sea to Split, where his predecessor was bishop.[36] There, in yet another of the throwbacks that make this period so fascinating, he was to live out his days in the palace of Diocletian. The UNESCO-protected city, seen in person today or in the eighteenth-century engravings of the Scottish architect Robert Adam, still has a distinctly Roman feel to it.[37]

The Ravenna that Orestes occupied on 28 August 475 had been there at Rome's beginning and it was there at the end. The city had been Julius Caesar's headquarters before he crossed the Rubicon in 50 BC. Its very impregnability had made it the perfect gilded cage in which to imprison political figures in the early empire. At the start of the first century it was home to, for example, Thusnelda, the wife of Arminius, who had wiped out three of Augustus' legions at Teutoburg Forest and stopped Roman thoughts of expansion across the River Rhine.

In some ways Ravenna was the perfect spot for a city. Certainly on late fifth-century coins it was called *Ravenna Felix, Fortunate Ravenna*. It was defendable and the gateway to Italy; just two of the reasons why, as we saw in the previous chapter, Honorius moved the Roman capital there at the start of the century. Yet we know of only one serious assault on the city in its early history – a naval attack during the civil wars in the first century BC. For the most part the city seems to have enjoyed a quiet life. The Roman geographer Strabo, for example, writes that the region was so healthy that Roman governors chose it as a spot to set up gladiatorial training camps. At full tide the sea washed away all the sewage. He also mentions that despite being situated on a marsh there was little chance of malaria or other diseases. It seems to have been a pleasant place to live. The beaches were sandy and good for riding, and gourmets raved about its turbot.[38]

The city's one major weakness, however, was a lack of drinking water. Passing through in 467, Sidonius Apollinaris complains that although there was water all around him, he could not quench his thirst. He paints an unsavoury picture of city walls stained with salt tide marks and swirls of mud as boats paddled along, the bottom stirred by the poles of bargemen. This was nothing new. Several centuries previously, acid as ever, the poet Martial commented that in the city he would rather have a cistern than a vine (the city had famously high-yielding vines) as he could sell his water there much better than any wine.[39]

But such infrastructural shortcomings were made up for by its logistical position. The attraction of Ravenna as a port had been recognised and exploited by the Emperor Augustus, who understood that with a fleet he could dominate the Mediterranean. As a partner to the military port he established at Misenum, near Naples, he constructed another, called Classis, on the Adriatic coast of Italy 3 kilometres or so south-east of Ravenna. Now the town of Classe, it was a first-class naval port in which was headquartered his eastern fleet. It was said in its heyday that the port could hold up to 250 ships in safe anchor, the harbour entrance illuminated by a lighthouse, just like the one at Alexandria.[40] The Classis fleet controlled the Adriatic Sea and

71

patrolled the Dalmatian coast, which had long been a centre of piracy. A visitor to Ravenna can get some sense of what the Roman port was like at the church of San Apollinare Nuovo in the town. One mosaic shows three ships entering the Byzantine harbour and two lighthouses at the entrance.

The best, certainly the most entertaining description of the city in which Romulus became emperor, is that of Sidonius Apollinaris, who, in another letter writes:

> In that marsh of yours the laws of everything are always the wrong way about; the waters stand and the walls fall, the towers float and the ships stick fast, the sick man walks and the doctor lies in bed, the baths are cold and the houses burn, the dead swim and the quick are dry, the powers are asleep and the thieves wide awake, the clergy live by usury and the Syrian chants the Psalms, business men turn soldiers and soldiers business men, old fellows play ball and young fellows hazard, eunuchs take to arms and rough allies to letters. And that is the kind of city you choose to settle in, a place that may boast a territory but little solid ground.[41]

For the next two months there is a strange silence in the West, almost as if it were drawing breath before its last gasp. Despite the intrinsic danger of seaborne travel, especially at that time of year, it is almost certain that diplomats would have been sailing back and forth to Byzantium to negotiate some kind of a peace agreement. If not that, then at the very least trying to achieve some kind of constitutional clarity. And if Julius Nepos was hoping for help from Constantinople, he was soon to find out that Emperor Zeno had problems of his own. In January 475, only three months after becoming emperor in name, he had been deposed by a conspiracy engineered by his own family and had to flee the capital. Zeno was not in fact to regain power until the following August. There was to be no help for Nepos from that quarter.

Finally, on 31 October 475, Orestes' son, the young teenager Romulus Augustus, was crowned emperor. There was certainly precedent for someone that youthful on the throne. The Emperor Valentinian III, for example, had been 6 when he had taken the purple fifty years earlier and, more recently, Leo II was 7 when he had become emperor of the East, the previous year.

Perhaps because we know his fate, it is natural to see portents of doom throughout Romulus' reign. The legend on his coins, 'D[ominus] N[oster] Romulus Augustus P[ius] F[elix] Aug[ustus]', standing for 'Our lord, Romulus Augustus, fortunate faithful Augustus', was too long for the engravers and on many that were struck the final word encroaches onto the image of the emperor. Looking at their work one has the sense almost as if the empire itself could no longer be bothered, though, to be fair, the coiners did have their work cut out.

There is no question that Romulus was a pubescent figurehead. More bluntly than most, one chronicler noted that Orestes 'undertook all the supervision of governmental affairs'.[42] He clearly had absolute power, so why did he not become emperor himself? The same chronicler also gives a reason, claiming that he did not do so because he was scared of eternal damnation. This seems unlikely. Certainly there was no real reason why Orestes could not assume the purple. He was not tainted with barbarian blood like Stilicho, nor was he an Arian like Ricimer. It seems more likely that he chose not to. The answer lies in the shift of power away from the purple. It made more sense, as Stilicho, Aetius and Ricimer had all recognised, to keep close to the army. Within living memory true control had always rested with emperor-makers, not the emperors. It is a sign not just where real authority lay, but where the status was. The more interesting questions to consider are what might Orestes have done had his

73

regime survived? What would the role have been for Romulus? Had he lived, Orestes would have moved into new political territory. There was no precedent there for him to follow. But sadly, neither question can be answered.

Romulus' reign started with some success, and there is no doubting his good intentions. He had the support of the senate. He was placatory to Byzantium too. Julius Nepos had broken off all contact with the East once Emperor Zeno had been overthrown, but Romulus played the appeaser, even minting coins in the name of Zeno's deposer. He inked a treaty with the Vandals in Africa, which must have been popular, protecting Italy as it did from their raids, and he seems to have made some peaceful overtures towards what was left of Gaul, which became secure enough for Arles to be one of the four mints used by Romulus (the others were Rome, Ravenna and Milan). But if Orestes had hoped that service with Attila gave him status with his own barbarian-dominated army, he was sadly mistaken. It became clear that this support was anything but widespread.

In the end, as befell so many of his predecessors, an army faction mutinied against its nominal head. It is an easy mistake to see the revolt against Orestes as a barbarian uprising, but it is important to remember that it was nothing of the kind. Initially at least, it was the uprising of the Roman army against its emperor. The events as presented by contemporary historians are a trifle confusing. Procopius gives us the most detailed account. He writes that the number of barbarians in the army had grown so large that Roman soldiers were oppressed and tyrannised by their barbarian comrades in arms. 'They [the barbarians] finally demanded that the Romans should divide with them the entire land of Italy. And indeed they commanded Orestes to give them the third part of this.'[43]

The army was dominated by a wide variety of barbarians, many of whom now wanted to settle down. The tradition of establishing them in Roman soil went back to the earliest days of the Republic. In the late 30s BC, Augustus' lieutenant Agrippa had relocated a group of German tribesmen across the River Rhine onto Roman territory around Cologne, and this had occurred on regular occasions throughout the history of the empire. More recently, both Honorius and Valentinian III had made several settlements in Gaul and Spain. It was Edeco's son Odovacer, head of the palace bodyguard, who petitioned on the army's behalf, having become its spokesman by the summer of 476.

However blunt the demands in Procopius are, the account reads considerably worse than it actually was. It is debatable how much land Odovacer and his army wanted. From what happened later, it seems as though what was actually meant by the Roman term *tertiae*, was in fact a third of the income that came from the land. Certainly that would account for the lack of mention of any land redistribution by contemporary authors or any sign of widespread dissent at the move. Given the skills which the Roman aristocracy had honed to avoid paying tax at all, as well as the number of estates they held throughout the empire, the actual impact on Italy may have been slight.[44]

The idea that Orestes was too attached to Italian aristocratic tradition to allow barbarians to soil hallowed ground, that essentially it was inveterate Roman snobbery that caused his downfall, has been much discussed yet has never had the air of plausibility about it. Apart from anything else, Orestes comes across as too much of a pragmatist. A modern historian has proposed a solution that rings much more true; that Orestes was already aware of the dangers that Odovacer posed to his power and that his refusal was political and personal rather than ideological.[45] It is, after all, extremely likely that Orestes and Odovacer had known each other for many years. At the time of the embassy to Constantinople in 449 for example, Odovacer would have been in his teens, not a great deal younger than Orestes himself.

Odovacer was head of the imperial bodyguard. He had been born in 433, so was in his early 40s when he rebelled. Sources remain vague about his ethnicity, a subject that seems to be of greater interest now than it was to Odovacer. Some call him a Goth, Rugian or Thuringian, others a Hun, one even a Saxon. The most reliable suggest that his father was a Hun, his mother a Scirian, an east Germanic tribe that eventually became Ostrogothic. The collapse of Attila's empire is the most likely reason why he did not boast about his father's ethnicity, that his mother was royalty the reason why he took hers. This is not as odd as it might seem – Ricimer had done exactly the same. The ethnic confusion among Roman writers is an indication that once you were a barbarian, it mattered little what type. It also points to the sheer variety of peoples that now made up the Roman army.

His childhood and young adulthood were dominated by the Huns. After Attila's death, Odovacer's father and brother Onoulf (probably slightly older than him) made a play for leadership of the Scirian tribe, but Edeco seems to have lost his life in battle in Pannonia in 469. His brother then made his way to Constantinople and entered imperial service. Odovacer seems not to have involved himself in family politics and had headed westwards before then. A glimpse has been preserved of a young Odovacer in the mid-450s, twenty years or more before he became ruler of Italy. He stopped to receive a blessing from St Severinus in Austria en route to Italy. Then in his mid- to late 20s, Odovacer is described as a gangly youth, dressed in shabby hides, having to stoop so that he does not bang his head on the ceiling of Severinus' cell. 'Leave here,' said the saint. Although now clothed in 'wretched hides', soon, he predicted 'you will distribute rich gifts to many'.[46]

When he reached Rome Odovacer appears to have risen rapidly through the ranks. He was soon a senior officer. History catches sight of him again in Rome in the early 470s. By 472 he was part of Anthemius' bodyguard, but supported Ricimer during his split with the emperor. It is a moot point whether he is mentioned because he was already important in his own right or because of what he was later to become. It is probably a mixture of the two. But from this time with Ricimer it is possible to see not only where Odovacer's experience and taste for power came from but also his support.

With Orestes' refusal to negotiate, it was clear that Italy would yet again be dragged into civil war. A meeting between what had effectively become the two sides was planned towards the end of August in Ticinum, the ancient name for Pavia. Although the city had fallen victim to Attila in 452, it remained a strategically significant town, in many ways the boundary to Italy proper. Pavia sat on the great highway that ran up from Rome. It was here that the Emperor Augustus met the funeral procession of his adopted son and heir, Drusus, after his death in Germany in 9 BC; it was here that Emperor Constantius II bid farewell to his nephew Julian the Apostate, en route to France soon after he had been promoted to Caesar. That it was rebuilt in the reign of Theodoric attests to its continued importance in late antiquity. Described by Procopius as a city with 'strong defences', it became one of the Gothic king's chief strongholds in the north of Italy, and the region's Fort Knox.[47]

Several days of negotiations ended with Orestes' continued refusal to bow to the army's demands. Frustrated and possibly with encouragement from Odovacer, the large number of observers, more accurately armed followers, rebelled. As the German historian Dirk Henning sadly notes, this type of putsch had been the 'norm rather than the exception' since the time of Valentinian III.[48]

An insight into the situation in Pavia is given by the man who was to become the town's bishop, Magnus Felix Ennodius, one of late antiquity's more neglected writers. Born in 473 of noble Gallic blood and brought up in Italy, he took holy orders in Pavia when he was in his early 20s. He accompanied Epiphanius, then the town's bishop, on his diplomatic mission in the spring of 475, and wrote his biography between 501 and 504. Ennodius gives a gripping account of what it was actually like inside Pavia. 'Vast hordes gathered within the city inflamed with a mad lust for booty,' he writes. There were riots, houses were set alight. Both churches were burned and the city 'glowed as if it were a funeral pyre'. The bishop's house was plundered and several hostages were taken, including Epiphanius' sister – though thanks to his experience as a diplomat he negotiated the release of all of them unharmed, his sister even before the day was out.[49]

Orestes had lost and the Scirian was proclaimed king, probably at Pavia, on 23 August. In his chronicle Cassiodorus writes: 'Odovacer assumed the title of king, using neither the purple nor the imperial regalia.'[50] The word 'king', *rex*, is crucial. Since the days of Tarquin the Proud it had struck fear into the hearts of right-minded Romans. Rome was never to have another emperor. This was the end of the empire.

It took just over a week for Odovacer to secure Italy. Orestes tried to escape but was captured and was unceremoniously dragged off to Placentia, modern Piacenza, where Avitus had been defeated. There are few Roman remnants to be seen in the city nowadays, but the orthogonal plan of the city centre alludes to the original military settlement. There Romulus' father was executed on 28 August. Romulus' uncle, Orestes' brother Paul, was captured, possibly trying to make his escape by boat. Certainly he was killed near Classis a few days later, either on 31 August or 4 September. Straight away, Odovacer entered Ravenna and captured both Romulus Augustulus and the throne.

As for Romulus, his fate was sealed. At the beginning of September, a week or so after his father's and uncle's executions, he was deposed. The chronicle the *Anonymous Valesianus* preserves the final moments of his reign:

> Then Odovacer entered Ravenna, deposed Augustulus from his throne, but in pity for his tender years, granted him his life; and because of his beauty he also gave him an income of 6,000 gold pieces and sent him to Campania to live there a free man with his relatives.[51]

THREE

To Be Beside the Seaside

As early as the end of the Roman Republic, the bay of Naples, the gulf that stretched from Cape Anthenaeum on the south up to Cape Misenum in the north was known as the 'bay of luxury' for its fashionable pleasure villas, summer homes for the Roman aristocracy. Its peaceful bay on which the rich could sail; its unrivalled views out to sea as far as the islands of Ischia and Capri; its inland lakes; and its hot springs where Roman matrons could take the sulphurous waters, all combined to make it the favourite Roman watering-hole. It was something of a gastronomic paradise, too. The sea off Cape Misenum was celebrated for its sea urchins, while nearby Baiae was famous for its abundant oysters.[1]

But, as happens to all fashionable destinations, a hint of snobbery began to emerge. The more accessible it became, the more people looked down their noses at it. Cattily, the poet Martial wrote that women would arrive in the region as a Penelope, the famously chaste wife of Odysseus, and leave a Helen, the much chased wife of Menelaus. In the first century, the philosopher Seneca wrote to a friend complaining that he had to leave Baiae the day after his arrival. He could not take any more of the dissolute mob: the drunks on the beach, loud parties on decorated pleasure boats, scantily clad women, endless singing and inebriated late-night brawling. It had not managed to shake off its disreputable image by the time of St Augustine, who referred to it as a place for degenerate pleasures, though it is hard to think who would ask a saint for holiday recommendations.[2]

81

Of course the Campanian coast was more than just a leisure destination, Rome's Blackpool. Misenum at the northern tip of the coast was the main naval station of the Mediterranean fleet, which at its height boasted 10,000 sailors. By the end of the first century, the commander in charge of Misenum was the equivalent of the British First Lord of the Admiralty or the US secretary of the navy – an administrator more than a soldier – and ranked above the various provincial fleets dotted around the empire. A sign of both the position's importance and the recognition of the value of sea power in the early days of the empire was that after Emperor Vespasian's accession in AD 69, the commander's salary was quintupled, from 60,000 sesterces to 300,000 sesterces. Some sense of the base's scale can be grasped today from the surviving rectangular water reservoir whose vaulted ceiling is supported by forty-eight pillars.[3]

One of the early commanders was Pliny the Elder, and it was from here that he launched the fleet that tried to save those threatened by the explosion of Mount Vesuvius in August AD 79, only to die in the process. In the fifth century, the naval base would not have held the 10,000 men that it had done in its heyday, but despite the inevitable decline, this was no provincial backwater.[4]

And it was here, at Misenum, on the promontory that looked over two seas, the Bay of Naples and the Bay of Gaeta, that Odovacer had condemned Romulus Augustulus to exile with his infamous honorarium of 6,000 gold *solidi* a year. The place itself is identified, in the words of the historian Jordanes, as the 'Castle of Lucullus in Campania'.[5] Much like Romulus' own name, that spot had a heritage that stretched back to the latter days of the Roman Republic and a long and involved history. Such was the extent of the building works there that for much of the Roman Empire what is generally called Lucullanum must have constituted most of the peninsula.

The castle, in the beginning a villa, had been built by the Roman politician Gaius Marius around the turn of the first century BC. It stood above and to the south-west of the naval site. In distinctly disapproving tones, the historian Plutarch notes in his biography of the man who had been consul a record seven times and had reformed the Roman army into the ruthlessly disciplined fighting machine that would take over the world, that Marius had designed a house that was too effete with an interior design much too luxurious. It was inappropriate, he suggested, for a man who had spent so much of his life on military campaigns and had seen too much action. This was not the universal view. A century later it was said to look like an army camp, and that Marius had used his military experience to make best strategic use of the view. All others were blind, compared to him, writes Pliny the Elder.[6]

Four years after Marius' death, the estate fell foul of the prescriptions of the greatest of Rome's Republican dictators, Lucius Cornelius Sulla, and into the hands of his eldest daughter, Cornelia Sulla. She paid the artificially depressed sum of only 75,000 sesterces for the house and land as an investment in AD 82. It is not too surprising that she made a huge profit when she sold it on, not long afterwards, when the property market recovered, for a massive 10 million sesterces. Over the previous decade, the Campanian coast had become one of Italy's property hot-spots and one of the first places where it is recorded that property had a value that went above and beyond its actual worth. It is here, too, that history meets Gaius Sergius Orata, the man who, in the 90s BC, has the dubious honour of being the first recorded estate agent. He would buy estates, fix them up with state-of-the-art baths and other refinements such as oyster beds, and then sell them on at a profit. Few either then or now will have mourned when he was sued by Cicero for misrepresenting the particulars on one estate.[7]

The man who bought the estate from Cornelia, Lucius Lucullus, was not a man of half-measures. A politician, a general and bon vivant (we have him to thank for the adjective 'lucullan'), he introduced the innovative spectacle of bulls fighting elephants to the circus and founded the first public libraries. A successful general in the East, he also holds a special place in the hearts of most gardeners: he was the man who introduced the cherry to the West, bringing it back from Asia. Lucullus' military career had been humiliatingly curtailed when he was asked to resign in favour of Pompey the Great in 66 BC. To compensate, he threw his energies into an expansive lifestyle, his name rapidly becoming a byword for luxury and indulgence. To give some indication of his wealth, after his death his fish alone fetched 4 million sesterces. But despite these undeniable over-the-top tendencies, Lucullus decided not to gild this particular lily any further.

This is not to say that a change of ownership found any more approval with the increasingly dour-sounding Plutarch. After he finishes describing the tunnels beneath the villa that brought in water for moats and fish ponds, he fails to find a Roman comparison extreme enough for what he thinks of Lucullus. He has to look to the degenerate East and ends up calling him a 'Xerxes in a gown'.[8]

Just like his famous Persian-style gardens in Rome, which were later regarded as among the richest of the imperial properties, Lucullus' house passed into imperial hands on his death in 56 BC, and inevitably then into those of the Emperor Tiberius. Augustus' successor appears to have visited the spot often and eventually died there at the age of 78 on 16 March AD 37. Intriguingly, an inscription dating to the period suggests that despite the imperial presence the villa continued to be known as Lucullus' villa, as indeed it was right up to and including the time of Romulus.

As a result of extensive damage and remodelling, as discussed below, only frustratingly small traces of the ancient villa of

Lucullanum can be seen. But across the bay at Stabiae at the base of Mount Vesuvius some sense can be had of what these pleasure palaces were like in their glory days. Excavated throughout the 1950s, the imposing Villa San Marco, for example – some 11,000 square metres – gives an indication of the scale of the building that was started during the reign of Augustus and appears to have been expanded under that of the Emperor Claudius. Looking at villas like this, it is clear that they had a relatively small number of private rooms, but of course it was their public rooms that were on show; elaborate colonnades, gardens, pools and dining-rooms that either overlooked the bay or were decorated with *trompe l'oeil* frescoes mimicking the real world. Another perspective of Romulus' new home can be gained by looking at the wall paintings depicting the region from sites of villas around the bay. These show ornate structures on several floors, steps down to the sea, curved porticos and artificial terracing.

In imperial hands, the villa Lucullanum survived the empire. In the fourth century it seems to have declined in importance, especially with eyes focused elsewhere in the empire. The Emperor Constantine gave some of its lands to the church in Naples, for example.[9] Sometime in the first half of the fifth century it gained an increasing number of fortifications. It is not recorded when this was, but it cannot be far wrong to date it to the 430s or 440s when the Vandals were harassing the coast of Italy. Presumably this remodelling is why Jordanes calls it the castle, not the villa of Lucullus.

Now called the Castel dell' Ovo, most of the massive fortress that stands on the islet of Borgo Marinaro – beautifully illuminated at night – dates to the seventeenth century. The castle owes its current name as much to its ovoid shape as to the medieval myth of the poet Virgil and an egg. In the Middle Ages, the author of the *Aeneid* had become a magician whose bones were said to protect the city of Naples. One alchemical legend has it that Virgil had an egg built, which was sealed in a flask and placed in an iron cage. Supported by silver ribbons, the cage was suspended from four columns on a round pillar of shaped bronze. The cage, flask and the egg were placed in a hidden chamber in the basement of the castle, where they were to stay if Naples was to remain safe.[10]

Few hints remain of the castle that Romulus would have known. There are some minor traces of the ancient villa in the chapel and some Roman columns, clearly reused, stand in the refectory, but these are more accidental survivors than useful pointers. The Normans and then the Angevins, who occupied the site in the twelfth and thirteenth centuries respectively, rebuilt extensively and, then, like much of Italy, the castle was bombed and destroyed at the end of the fifteenth century. Thereafter, in swift succession it was occupied by the French and then the Spaniards, who rebuilt it as it looks today.

It is here, in this spot, that the story of Romulus Augustulus traditionally ends. Forever young, forever beautiful, he remains for us frozen in time in Lucullanum. It satisfies from both a narrative and a historical point of view. There had been a tradition of emperors withdrawing to the country to see out their days. Septimus Severus spent most of his final years on the Campanian coast; Diocletian retired from office to tend his cabbages on the Dalmatian coast; the Emperor Hadrian died in a villa at Baiae; and, as noted above, the Emperor Tiberius had even died in this very castle. The great classical historian J.B. Bury notes how the names of this period meet the reader in the pages of the chroniclers 'like ghosts re-arisen from past days of Roman history'.[11] With the last emperor in his villa, the story has come full circle.

On a more individual level, there is also a sense of relief that Romulus survived the empire in 'opulent obscurity', as one historian has it.[12] Anyone reading around this period needs a strong stomach and soon becomes numbed to the Tarantinoesque levels of gore. Of the eight Western emperors who came between Valentinian III and Romulus Augustulus, two were murdered, probably stabbed; one was strangled; one was possibly poisoned; one was butchered by his slaves and had his dismembered body thrown in the Tiber; one was arrested, stripped, beaten and beheaded; and only two, as far as we can tell, died natural deaths. That Romulus' abdication ended without bloodshed provides a momentary pause before the next round of politicking and civil warfare.

But that is by no means the end of the story. Romulus Augustulus did not spend the rest of his days on an isolated estate, bitterly pondering, as many would have him, what might have been. The last emperor did not become an eccentric aristocratic anachronism, like a retired former British imperial governor back in the home country, staring increasingly myopically and with growing incomprehension at the world around him from his cottage in Sussex, penning vitriolic letters to *The Times*. Although the position of former emperor is not a common one, for better modern analogies we need to look East, either to Mr Pu-Yi, the last emperor in China's Forbidden Palace, potting his plants in the Beijing Botanical Gardens, or Emperor Hirohito of Japan, the former god who reinvented himself as a marine biologist.

It is possible to get some idea of what it was that happened to Romulus when he became a private citizen. The reconstruction that follows was first proposed at the end of the nineteenth century and has grown in credence since it was examined in convincing detail in the early 1990s.[13]

Above all, the idea that Romulus was sent into exile in Misenum should not give the impression of bucolic isolation, cut off from what was happening elsewhere in Italy. It is possible even that Romulus was almost as much in the thick of it, at least as a silent observer, as he had been in Ravenna. By now, Lucullanum had become something of a military and administrative centre. It was still partly owned by the state and there are hints that it had a political role, though there is too little information for this to be understood in any greater detail. We do know that after it had passed out of imperial and into Gothic hands, in some sense the estate became a bureaucratic enclave, housing retired civil servants. A diplomat in Africa was honoured with land there, as was one of Theoderic's generals after a successful campaign in Gaul. The point is that this was not the place where people were sent to keep them out of the way.[14]

By the 490s, when Romulus would have been in his early 30s, Lucullanum was home to a significant monastery associated with the cult of St Severinus. Geoffrey Nathan, the academic who has studied this subject in the greatest depth, raises two important questions. First, is there a connection between Romulus and Severinus? Second, what links Severinus and Naples?[15]

A clue is offered in that Romulus Augustulus seems to have taken holy orders. But to answer these questions properly, it is worth digressing for a moment to look at St Severinus, partly because an understanding of the saint's life and his connection to Romulus and his family sheds light on the emperor's career, and partly because the saint lived out his life for the most part against a background of the collapsing province of Noricum. More accurately, Noricum Ripense, which fell within the boundaries of what is, broadly speaking, modern Austria, is, as mentioned in the introduction, a perfect counter for those who favour the settlement theory of the decline of the Roman Empire.

The saint's life, written in 511 by his former pupil Eugippius, provides an unparalleled picture of a province hanging on to civilisation by its fingernails. Severinus was aware that something was threatening the empire, that society was declining and about to vanish. The simile that Eugippius uses, in all likelihood from Severinus himself, is that of the biblical Exodus. Like the departure of the Jews for the promised land from Egypt, so too any Romans who were left would have to move to Italy if they wanted to avoid 'the unjust rule of the barbarians', he warned.[16]

What makes the province of Noricum such a fascinating example is that it was slightly off the beaten track. It was not on any major trade or military route, it had no unique resources, it was in many ways the average province that had grown up, as Peter Heather writes, 'about one part central planning to eight parts local initiative'. Initially, at least, its decline was gradual. There was no sign of the extreme collapse that was witnessed in Britain, and it took most of the fifth century to fall over.

Archaeologists reckon that coin circulation had pretty much expired not only within the interior of the province, but even on the Danubian forts by around 400. It is especially marked around Salzburg, where we see the end of villa culture in the countryside. It is only at Lorch that a relatively large number of coins of a later date have been found. Understandably, the troops, without any kind of regular income, began to disperse. The death knell was sounded for the province in the middle of the century when Attila passed through Noricum en route to Gaul. His was only the first of several barbarian invasions that gave the locals no chance to recover.

Most significantly, the Rugians, an east Germanic tribe which was later to cause difficulties for Romulus' successor, settled just beyond the north-eastern border of Noricum and forced Mautern and other cities to pay it tribute. That the negotiations for this tribute were organised by the cities themselves is a clear indication that all was not well. It would have been unthinkable treachery for individuals to sign any kind of a surrender or allow barbarians on Roman soil without the express permission of Rome.

By the time that Severinus appeared in Noricum the Roman administration was effectively at an end. There was no governor, no military commander and what little defence existed, was organised by individual townships. The saint appeared in Asturis in the mid-450s (the town has not been identified though it has been linked with both Zwentendorf and Zeiselmauer) from somewhere in the Middle East, where he had been for the past few years. As with the anonymous cowboy in a Hollywood western appearing out of the mist, riding into town and promising protection and salvation, we know nothing of his background. Eugippius is frustratingly and deliberately vague on the subject – as presumably Severinus was himself – though there is a definite implication that he was an aristocrat.[17]

Severinus eventually settled in Mautern, his base for the next twenty years until his death in 482. What is left of the walls on the west side of the former Roman camp are some of the most impressive remains in Lower Austria; the ruin of the watchtower, built in the first century and strengthened in the fourth, is an indication of the frontier nature of the town.

Severinus' religious work against pagans and heretics apart, the picture that emerges is of a talented diplomat and administrator trying to protect the people in the province as best he could in the face of impossible odds – to keep some life pumping through the veins of a collapsed infrastructure. Severinus made numerous moves to keep barbarian raiders out of the province, to have hostages released when they were captured, while at the same time trying to organise basic food and supplies by imposing tithes. At no point did Severinus have any specific authority for what he did, either within the Church or more broadly in civil society. What status he had was achieved by his own charisma and talents. And it is clear that this was formidable: his reputation travelled well beyond Roman society, not just to the nearby Rugians, but even further afield.

The most apparent side-effect of the frequent barbarian incursions was that the local economy was in an unimaginably bad state. The locals themselves had little impetus to consider any long-term plans. It requires scant imagination to guess with what little enthusiasm the people of Noricum still ploughed the fields or bothered to plant seeds at all. Some trading links with the outside world did remain, though they were in a fractured state. Oil was imported, albeit, writes Eugippius, with great difficulty, and some examples of pottery from Africa, datable to the second half of the fifth century, have been found in Mautern.[18]

This is not to say that there was no wealth left in the province at all. Eugippius mentions an aristocratic widow near Mautern who had both enough land and enough space to hoard grain so that she could push up prices (Severinus shamed her into sharing). And some elaborate mosaics of this period have been found in the cemetery church in Teurnia, now St Peter in Holz, and at Hemmaberg, though admittedly they are slightly further south. But these are isolated instances. The overwhelming impression from the pages of Eugippius is one of poverty, starvation and increasing isolation.

The people of Noricum began to realise how exposed they were to barbarian raids, and so moved away from their villas and towns into self-fortified towns – the German word for them, *Fliehburgen*, is often used – guarded by citizen militias with scouts keeping an eye open for raiders. These settlements, typically on protected high ground and out of the way, were intended as permanent living spots as well as shelters to see out the latest raid.

One of the best examples is the 2.7-hectare site of Lavant-Kirchbichl in the Tirol, some 2 kilometres east of Lienz, and south of the River Drau. Inhabited from the beginning of the fifth century, presumably after the destruction of Lienz in 407, it was evidently an important site. It boasts two churches dating from

91

this period, one of which, it became apparent during excavations in the early 1950s, was a cathedral. The site had been picked for defence. It was difficult to get to, bounded to the east and west by streams and to the south by a deep ravine. Access was only from the north and the hill itself is over 800 metres high. Indeed, so secure was the site that few traces of walls have been found – they simply were not needed. As they excavated, archaeologists began to reckon that this had been a permanent move rather than temporary shelter in times of trouble. This was confirmed in the 1980s with the discovery of three houses with hypocaust underfloor heating.

The importance of the settlement, clearly a significant religious and therefore administrative centre, is offset slightly by the simplicity of the finds. These reveal a mostly agrarian people, certainly a self-contained one. Numerous bobbins and loom weights point to the manufacture of wool and linen; there are traces of iron working (such as a furnace), and bone analysis indicates the presence of cattle, pigs, horses, goats, sheep and chickens. But decorative objects are few and far between.

Severinus encouraged the people of Noricum to move to these fortified towns and bring all their possessions with them, telling them to put their faith in walls. This way, he said, if there were an invasion, the barbarians would have no one to raid and they would then be forced 'to abandon their frightful and cruel designs'.[19] There was no relying on the military: that was non-existent. Mautern was left with a solitary tribune called Mamertinus, and no weapons – these had melted away, along with the troops. Although this had been by no means a rapid procedure – it had taken a couple of generations – it became apparent that the people of Noricum were less and less able to rely on any kind of outside help.

Eugippius catches the violence of the moment with a horrible anecdote of the other remaining garrison, that at Passau. Some soldiers from this barracks, he writes, had gone to Italy to fetch the final remittance for their comrades. It was their pay-off before they disbanded themselves. Unknown to their companions who had stayed behind, they were all massacred en route:

> One day, as Saint Severinus was reading in his cell, he suddenly closed the book and began to sigh deeply and to weep. He ordered those around him to run quickly to the River Inn, which he stated was then and there crimson with human blood. At that moment, word was brought that the bodies of the soldiers mentioned above had been washed ashore by the river's current.[20]

In Severinus' latter years, Noricum was faced with more and more disasters. From the 470s onwards there seemed to be little good news as town after town fell. When Joviacum, either present-day Schlögen or Aschach, was destroyed, Eugippius adds only the gory detail that the priest Maximianus was hanged on a cross.[21] In a last-ditch attempt at protecting his flock, Severinus evacuated the settlements upstream from Lorch into the town. This move seems to have given the region a brief respite. When Lorch was besieged, the barbarians were repulsed – all they got away with was a herd of cattle. But it proved to be all-too brief a victory: soon Lorch was lost as well.

Severinus himself died in Mautern on 8 January 482. A sign of how temporary his protection had been is that not even his remains were able to rest in peace. As the Rugians continued their sorties across the Danube into Noricum they even sacked the monastery where he was buried. They took everything, only leaving the walls, Eugippius writes sardonically, because they could not be carried across the Danube.[22] By 488 the inevitable had to be faced. Noricum had to be abandoned.

Even though Severinus had proved ultimately unsuccessful, trying to halt the barbarian torrent with an umbrella, the Norican survivors were unwilling to leave their mentor and protector in the hands of the sacrilegious barbarians. As they left their homeland, their province, they took Severinus' remains with them. His body, which, as in the stories of all saints, was found to be incorrupt, was brought from Noricum to Italy in a horse-drawn wagon, ending its journey at a castle in Macerata di Montefeltre, near Urbino.

This is where Romulus' mother Barbaria re-enters the story. Evidently a bright, literate, wealthy, strong-willed and devout woman, she was now in her mid-40s. Her and her husband's connection with Noricum have been mentioned in the previous chapter, and are circumstantially confirmed by their relationship with St Severinus. Eugippius comments that both of them 'had a great devotion' for Severinus, and corresponded with him.[23]

Barbaria was clearly a feisty woman. She had already had to cope with the death of her husband and brother-in-law; several moves around Italy; the uncertainty of her own fate; as well as concern over her surviving son. The sources are too limited to flesh out the impression in any great detail, but she seems to have thrown herself into the Church. With the abandonment of Noricum and the transfer of Severinus' remains to Italy, she clearly wanted to devote her energies to building his memorial. At the end of the 480s or early 490s she spent time petitioning and canvassing Church officials and the rest of the congregation in Misenum.

Sometime soon thereafter, certainly within the pontificate of Gelasius (by 496 at the latest), she received authorisation from Rome to move the saint's remains to Lucullanum for permanent burial. This permission raises a number of unanswerable questions both about Romulus and his mother's status within society and Odovacer's view of his predecessor. Did the Scirian ever think there might be a use for Romulus? Was the former emperor being kept on the reserve bench in case Zeno tried to field a different candidate? Did Odovacer save Romulus out of respect for his family? Odovacer had, after all, met the saint. Did he even encourage the family's interest in the cult of St Severinus? Why was the mother of someone who had been forced to abdicate at sword-point perceived as so small a threat that she was allowed to travel around the region and petition officials?

There, in a mausoleum Barbaria had built in Lucullanum, the local bishop, Victor, buried the saint in a ceremony that was attended by the whole town. The construction of this crypt is a plausible outlet for the 6,000 *solidi* a year that had been granted to Romulus. It is possibly out of gratitude for this that the reference to Romulus' father in Eugippius' writings is flattering. Although the allusion is oblique, there is a distinctly partisan tone when the bishop refers, in the introduction of the *Life of St Severinus*, to Orestes' 'unjust murder'.[24]

That Romulus Augustulus went into the Church is not at all surprising. Aristocratic involvement with the Church had a long tradition in the Roman Empire. Over a century earlier, in the 340s, even the future Emperor Julian was to be seen rebuilding the church of St Mamas in Turkey. Perhaps inevitably because of his later apostasy, wrote hostile Church historians, the church fell down (though this is not too surprising in what is, after all, an area known for earthquakes).[25] Holy orders remained an honourable occupation for the wealthy lay person in the fifth and sixth centuries.

More specifically, in the fifth century the Church had proved to be the compassionate option for those removed from the throne. Enforced or voluntary ordination foreshadows what was later to become standard Byzantine practice.[26] When he was forcibly retired by Julius Nepos, the former Emperor Glycerius became bishop of Split, while several years earlier the Emperor Avitus had become bishop of Placentia.

Eugippius, abbot of the monastery in Lucullanum, and writing, as mentioned, in 511, comments on the cult that grew up around the mausoleum. 'A monastery, built at the same place to the memory of the blessed man, still endures,' he says.[27] Under Eugippius' rule, Romulus' place of exile flourished. The monastery had a decent library and was one of the literary centres of Italy at the time. Before his death in 538, Eugippius himself compiled the first anthology of the works of St Augustine, a blockbuster that weighs in at 1,000 pages; the monastery's manuscript of Jerome's Vulgate translation of the Bible into Latin was used twenty years later by Cassiodorus for the revision which appeared in the seventh volume of his own nine-volume Bible; and there are references to copies of letters of St Augustine and to several works by the theologian Tyrannius Rufinus.

Lucullanum remained a centre of sorts for several hundred years. Pope Gregory the Great mentions it on a number of occasions as a spot of some importance, and its reputation had grown so much that by the eighth century it had become a place of pilgrimage. A Saxon pilgrim, the Wessex-born St Willibald, visited it in 729 on the way back from a pilgrimage to the Holy Land. It was not until the start of the tenth century, with the Saracen threat to Campania, that the monastery began what was a terminal decline. In 902 Severinus' remains were moved to Naples to preserve them from this threat, and finally again in 1807 to Frattamaggiore around 11 kilometres outside the city, where they remain to this day.[28]

With Orestes dead and Romulus and his mother involved with church works, out of the way in Misenum, what was happening to Odovacer? Now that he was king, the first challenge the

Scirian had to face was that of securing his own position, which was by no means as secure as might be thought. The vague hints that we have indicate conspiracies at a high level within the barbarian command. One chronicle states baldly that the king killed a certain Count Brachila (definitely not a Roman name) at Ravenna. Another historian corroborates the story, adding the strange twist that the count was killed to inspire fear in the Romans – an example of how he would treat other traitors. The following year we hear that another nobleman was executed along with his mother and brother. These literary accounts of unhappiness are confirmed archaeologically by a horde of Germanic and Roman jewellery that was buried for safety in Reggio Emilia in northern Italy, and which belonged to a clearly wealthy man called Ettila and his wife Stafara.[29]

But if his own Germanic tribesmen were unhappy and not adverse to plotting his overthrow, it is curious that the same cannot be said of the Romans in Italy. Certainly there is no indication of any kind of organised Roman resistance to Odovacer's rule, which suggests that the regime was not as oppressive as the land claims and execution of Count Brachila would suggest. Indeed, we know of only one man, an aristocratic clergyman called Primenius who fled out of Italy heading for Noricum, scared at what Orestes' murderers might do to him. But this clearly has nothing to do with barbarian rule per se. Primenius appears to have been a mentor to Romulus' father, and presumably his fears were specific and personal. Nonetheless his flight does imply an uncertainty, at least a perceived question mark, over Romulus' fate and that of his supporters in the opening moments of Odovacer's reign.

As for Odovacer's rule, it is true that little changed for the worse once he had the reins of power in his hands. It was a startlingly smooth takeover. If anything, the Scirian introduced a note of stability to Italy that had been missing under the shadow emperors.

Broadly speaking, his thirteen years of rule, from 476 to 489, were an oasis of peace. Certainly Cassiodorus' later snipes at Odovacer's 'degraded reign' should be taken with a pinch of salt.[30]

We have seen that Romulus and his mother were treated with respect, a courtesy that seems to have been the hallmark of his reign. He listened to the senate, which in turn rewarded him with its support. It is true, of course, that the land settlement that had caused his revolt against Orestes in the first place was not popular, but as mentioned in the previous chapter, it is questionable to what extent it was actually implemented.

Odovacer also seems to have achieved broader popular support by proving to be magnanimous when he needed to be. Epiphanius, for example, managed to negotiate a five-year tax break for Pavia from Odovacer to ease the cost of rebuilding the city after his struggle for power with Orestes, and the Scirian also revoked a sentence of exile for a friend of Severinus. Furthermore, there was no persecution of the Church. His reign was a time of religious tolerance, despite the fact that he was an Arian. In foreign affairs, too, Odovacer seems to have been sound and unsurprisingly conciliatory towards other barbarians. Although he may have lost Provence fairly soon after he had taken power, he did manage to get back Sicily from the Vandals (admittedly at a small financial cost). It was a small price to pay. Not only will this have brought much-needed tax revenue from Sicilian estates back into the exchequer, but stabilising the Mediterranean will have increased trade.

A sign of the general economic upswing of Italy at the time can be seen at San Giovanni di Ruoti, a villa in the highlands of Lucania in southern Italy. After an earthquake in 460, it was not just rebuilt but remodelled and on a much grander scale, with large halls and a bath house. New buildings were added, a lookout tower and a domed entrance. Most impressively of all, it also gained a stunning polychrome mosaic-decorated dining hall.

And sign too of increasing Mediterranean security can be seen in the number of imports from North Africa.[31]

In all this it is a shock to realise how much Odovacer had gone native. His thought and behaviour was now Roman. There was no question at all of replacing what he had found when he took control with a barbarian command structure. Procopius goes to great pains to write that Theoderic 'preserved both the laws and the form of government as strictly as any who have been Roman emperors'.[32] Exactly the same could be said of Odovacer. He was adapting to Rome rather than Rome to him.

One question about Odovacer's rule has dominated academic discussion: what was his position? Was he an independent king? A viceroy, governing Italy in Zeno's name? Was he both at the same time; a German king to the barbarians, Zeno's officer to the Romans? This is, it must be admitted, a complicated, technical debate. Few of the arguments have taken into consideration the duplicitous nature of diplomacy; that it is sometimes necessary to say one thing and mean another and that at other times it can be in everyone's interest not to ask too many questions.

Perhaps a more pertinent and useful line of questioning, at least one for which we can essay answers, is what did Odovacer wish to be? It is clear that he wanted to be seen as more than just a barbarian leader. It was the need for some kind of formal acknowledgement of the power he had appropriated that had led him to send the senatorial embassy to Byzantium, as detailed in the Introduction. What is interesting is the clear value he placed on having a Roman title – being accepted, as it were, by the establishment. This seems to have been more than a usurper craving official recognition: it is almost as if he wanted to be a Roman. So when the Emperor Zeno granted him the title of patrician, it made him, in his own eyes at least, the successor of Stilicho, Aetius, Ricimer and indeed Orestes. It has been argued that the title was meaningless as it gave him no actual power. That is missing the point. Odovacer had no need of the power, which he already had. He was an outsider wanting to be part of the club: it was the title he craved.

Possibly the best indication of how much Odovacer valued his benediction from the East is that right up until the end of his reign he was careful to avoid any kind of *lèse-majesté*. For the most part he shunned any kind of title at all. All official documents were dated in the name of the consul. On his coins he is presented bare-headed and no imperial regalia is displayed; on a public inscription, commemorating his sponsorship of the Coliseum's renovation, he calls himself simply 'most excellent Odovacer' (to be more accurate, the precise word is lost, but it is clear that there is no intention of kingship there).

He himself may have used the titles with care, but confusion remained and the water is muddied by the historians of the period. Sometimes he is called king pure and simple, at others his title is qualified with the name of some tribes. A point worth considering is to what extent this was deliberate. The inscription in the Coliseum could easily be self-consciously modest. Odovacer could play at being the private citizen, but then private citizens did not generally erect inscriptions in so public a place. Another inscription, set up by a member of the senate, refers to 'our lord Zeno and the lord Odovacer'. It must have been a much-debated phrase. One could of course read into this – and I am sure that this is deliberate – that Odovacer was on a similar level to Zeno; but the wording is as vague in Latin as it is in English.[33]

From Zeno's point of view, this seems to have suited him so long as it was agreed that Rome and Italy were still part of the Roman Empire. Whatever his private thoughts on the subject might have been, he was playing with a bad diplomatic hand. There was no question whatsoever of invading Italy and placing Julius Nepos on the throne once more. As long as Odovacer had an army and held Italy, Nepos could claim as much sovereignty as he wanted. Odovacer was the real ruler and no one should ask too many questions. Certainly after the embassies disappeared from Constantinople there is no mention of a second round of negotiations or any kind of a resumption of talks. The essential ambiguity was fine as long as it did not threaten the East. And in any case, Zeno had far too many worries of his own to waste time with the West.

This deliberately confused status quo was maintained until the murder of Julius Nepos in 480. On 25 April, 9 May or 22 June of that year – the sources disagree – the former emperor was assassinated, 'pierced by unexpected blows' in his villa outside the city by his own supporters. There are whispers that Bishop Glycerius, the emperor he had deposed, was involved, but they are no more than the faintest hint. News of the incident, which will have sailed quickly across the Adriatic Sea, must have caused Romulus Augustulus some concern. He will not have been the only one to have noticed that deposed emperors had a nasty habit of dying soon after their removal from office. It might have been some consolation to the teenager that after Nepos' murder Odovacer pursued the assassins. This had the effect both of making him look good and of regaining Dalmatia.[34]

Come 486, however, a decade after he had deposed Romulus, Odovacer's house of cards began to wobble unsteadily, although this was not to become apparent for another couple of years. Romulus' successor, as John Moorhead points out, was doomed 'by an obscure series of events in the east and the north'.[35]

It is fair to say that however much they had tolerated each other, relations between Odovacer and Zeno had never been warm. The flashpoint was some form of communication – the term 'conspiracy' is much too strong a word – which appears to have taken place between Odovacer and Illus, the last of the generals to have plotted against the Emperor Zeno several years before.

After a couple of (state-sponsored) assassination attempts designed to curb Illus' apparent ambitions for power, at the end of 481 the general had moved out of Zeno's and dagger's reach to Antioch. Within a few years he had put together plans for a revolution and had picked a pretender to the throne to be his figurehead. Illus eventually took the field near Antioch, where he was soundly beaten by an imperial force. He and his puppet escaped, were eventually betrayed and beheaded, after which their heads were brought to Byzantium where they rotted away on spears for all to see.

His revolt had prompted Illus to ask the West – Odovacer – for assistance. Although there is no evidence that Odovacer even so much as replied, let alone offered to support him, the request alone appears to have been enough to damn him in the emperor's eyes.

Zeno managed to encourage the Rugians, close allies in previous campaigns, to assault Italy. Odovacer found out and launched a successful pre-emptive strike in 487 in which the Rugian king and queen were taken and executed. The following year, Odovacer's brother wiped out the remaining Rugian power by defeating the king's son.

Collateral damage in this international game of chess was the total destruction of Noricum. What the campaign had made clear was that the province could no longer be defended. Odovacer had neither the resources nor the appetite for a further military operation there. He gave the order to abandon the province, all land between the Alps and the Danube. Not even lip service could now be paid to Roman rule north of the Alps.

Although life carried on in Noricum, it bore little resemblance to what had gone on before. In his history of the province, the historian and archaeologist Géza Alföldy concludes: 'This continuity of occupation was connected at most only to a very limited degree with any continuity in the Romanised population; and there was no continuity at all in the corporate organisation of the community.'[36] By no stretch of the imagination can what happened in Noricum be described as a peaceful transition.

There is a sense that an awareness of Zeno's long arm and the implications of his displeasure made Odovacer rather nervous. His international moves now were not just placatory, they were positively deferential towards Byzantium. The Scirian set up a statue of Zeno on a horse, made of bronze and covered in gold, in Ravenna. It was so beautiful that Charlemagne later stole it and had it set up in his palace in Aachen. And after his victory over the Rugians, Odovacer acted out the role of a traditional general fighting for his emperor. Throughout the history of the empire all victory marches, triumphs through the capital, were done in the name of the emperor: indeed, victories were recorded in the name of the emperor. By sending some of the booty he had captured from the Rugians to Zeno, Odovacer was emphasising his subservient and loyal position as the mouthpiece of the emperor in the West.[37]

The forelock tugging failed to work. Zeno had decided on invasion, a plan that would rid him of two problems at once. There was later a tradition that the emperor's decision was retributive, to punish Odovacer for his unjust treatment of Romulus.

Accordingly, [Zeno] persuaded Theoderic, our ruler, although he was on the point of besieging him and Byzantium, not only to put an end to his hostility towards himself, in recollection of the honour which Theoderic had already received at his hands in having been made a patrician and consul of the Romans, but also to punish Odovacer for his unjust treatment of Romulus Augustulus, and thereafter, in company with the Goths to hold sway over the land as its legitimate and rightful rulers.

This however, sounds like convenient gossip after the fact, rather than a genuine point of view.[38]

Zeno's agent in the attack was a young 36-year-old Ostrogoth called Theoderic, about whom we shall read more in the following chapter. In one fell swoop, encouraging Goth against Goth, the emperor had got rid of both the Ostrogoths, who had been causing difficulties in the Eastern empire, and his hangnail in the West, Odovacer. What made Zeno's moves even more dishonourable is that the Eastern emperor kept his options open. His acceptance of Odovacer's nomination for consul in 490 was an attempt, later unneeded, to keep lines of communication open there. This cynical approach to foreign policy was typical and not unexpected. In his *Byzantine History*, Malchus of Philadelphia reports a conversation between two Gothic leaders: 'Whichever of us falls, they [Byzantium] will be the winners with none of the effort.'[39]

Theoderic's intentions towards Italy were permanent. This was to be no raiding mission or punitive affair. Given the vast number of people and possessions involved, ships were out of the question. Setting out after harvest time, he had reached the Adriatic Sea towards the end of 488 accompanied by, so noted one author, 'the whole world' – a vast number of Goths, women, children, livestock, together with all of their portable possessions crammed onto wagons. Some (there is vague consensus) 100,000 of them made the journey. The Ostrogoths were coming to stay.[40]

By the spring of the following year Theoderic had made it round the top of the Adriatic, like a lion in the middle of a herd, writes one contemporary. Even though it is implausible that Odovacer cannot have realised what Theoderic's intentions were by this stage, the Ostrogoth remained unmolested and kept gaining on Odovacer's territory. When he did, it was momentous. As James O'Donnell points out: 'The ensuing Italian war was not a noble or uplifting experience for anyone.' Odovacer was first defeated on the banks of the Isonzo river, not far from the ruins of Aquileia, on 28 August. The size of Theoderic's force must have terrified Odovacer, however much notice he had had of the Ostrogothic advance.[41]

A month later, on 27 September, Odovacer was defeated once more. He had retreated and dug his forces into Verona, a strategically important city that oversaw the road from the Brenner Pass. It was one of those desperate battles, the traces of which have left virtually no imprint on the human memory. But so heavy were the losses that bones still lay on the ground eighteen years later, trampled over by foraging cattle.[42] Faced with this second defeat, Odovacer decided to split his army. He himself sought sanctuary and headed southwards towards Ravenna, the rest of his army marched westwards to Milan.

The year was not yet out, however. After several more bloodless successes, the surrender of several cities and the apparent defection of Odovacer's deputy, Theoderic could have been forgiven for thinking that he had won Italy in little under a year. But this campaign was to continue right through the winter. Odovacer took the field once more and reversed some of Theoderic's gains. His biggest coup was convincing his recalcitrant deputy to re-defect and, as a result, he captured a number of Theoderic's senior officers who were clapped in chains and sent to Ravenna.

As winter approached, the war continued. While Odovacer returned to Ravenna, Theoderic and his army billeted themselves in Pavia. For those who lived through this enforced occupation, these were undoubtedly 'trying days'. Ennodius writes: 'One saw the city teeming with family groups and the heads of great houses forced to take shelter in narrow huts. One saw huge buildings crowded to the point of starting from their very foundations, while not even the ground itself sufficed to bear the weight of that dense population.'[43]

Throughout this, Bishop Epiphanius protected his people, making sure that hostages were released without ransom. Then after this 'sad and destructive war', he rebuilt and repopulated the city again.

As 489 became 490, Italy had effectively been partitioned. In this stalemate, both Theoderic and Odovacer made very different political moves. The former bought time by sending an embassy to Byzantium, a deference to the East he reinforced by issuing coins in Zeno's name. An indication of quite how much weight he placed on Byzantium's approval is that the head of the mission was quite deliberately the last man to serve as consul before 476, in other words the last authentic consul. Odovacer, on the other hand, had had enough of playing Uriah Heep. He started minting coins without any mention at all of the Eastern emperor and named Thela, his own young son, Caesar. The implications of this will not have gone unnoticed. It was Odovacer's final break from Byzantium. Apart from the fact that the authority to name a Caesar could only come from an emperor, he was treading rather too closely in the footsteps of Orestes.

Odovacer was beaten a third and, in retrospect, bloodily conclusive time, on 11 August at the Adda river, a tributary of the River Po, in northern Italy. His power pretty much broken, he fled to Ravenna, where he found himself blockaded. Theoderic and his army camped 5 kilometres east of the city in Pineta, where Romulus' uncle Paul had been executed. The small palace Theoderic apparently used during this time has been partially excavated outside Ravenna's city walls at Santa Maria di Palazzolo.[44]

With Odovacer safely isolated, Theoderic could concentrate on cleaning up the rest of Italy. Yet one should not be distracted by the benefit of hindsight. The siege was by no means a foregone conclusion. Untouchable in impregnable Ravenna, Odovacer made frequent armed sorties out of the city to harass the Goths at night. 'This not once or twice, but often,' writes Jordanes.[45] These raiding parties may have done much for morale within the city, but they did not advance Odovacer's position in any material way, and so he planned one last attempt to break out. At the beginning of July (the evening of the 9th) the 60-year-old Odovacer himself led a band of Germanic warriors, we are told Heruli, to attack Theoderic's camp. It was an unmitigated disaster. There were huge losses on both sides and Odovacer's fickle deputy was killed.

From this point forward there is a sense that Theoderic had decided to finish the matter once and for all. Certainly his blockade of the port from the end of August was the final straw for those in the city. With resentment growing within Ravenna, fanned by food shortages (the price of grain, notes one source, had risen so that a gold piece bought only 2⅔ pints of wheat[46]), Odovacer eventually capitulated in February 493 and the gates of Ravenna were opened on 5 March after the Scirian had handed over his son as a hostage to Theoderic.

The terms of the agreement as they are reported appear bafflingly naive. The plan seems to have been that Theoderic and Odovacer live side-by-side, on equal terms, and rule over Italy together. This had rarely worked on an imperial scale and it is impossible to imagine how anyone could possibly have thought that this would work within a single territory. Of course it did not. Suspiciously soon afterwards – within ten days – Theoderic got news of an assassination plot, either imagined or real (both are plausible). When Odovacer came to Theoderic's head-quarters, he was jumped and held down by two of the Goth's henchmen. Then, sword drawn, Theoderic himself stepped up.

The Greek seventh-century historian John of Antioch preserves what happened next. Odovacer's gnomic question to his attacker was 'Where is my God?' Less opaquely Theoderic replied: 'This is what you did to my friend,' referring to his execution of the

Rugian royal family, before he cut him through in a mighty sword stroke from collarbone to hip. As he died, the Goth quipped 'There certainly wasn't a bone in this blasted man's body.'[47] Although Odovacer was honoured with a grave – a stone coffin – the rest of his family and senior officers were massacred in brutal and bloody fashion. His brother tried for sanctuary in a church but was shot down in a hail of arrows; his wife was imprisoned and starved to death. Like Romulus, Odovacer's son was arrested and exiled, though Thela seems to have had imperial pretensions after all: he escaped back to Italy, where he was killed.

The man who had eradicated Rome's final kingmaker now himself suffered the same fate.

FOUR

No More Heroes

When the army of the Eastern emperor, led by the brilliant General Belisarius, was invading Italy in the 530s, the then Gothic king, nephew to Theoderic, asked a famous Jewish soothsayer to predict the outcome of the war. The king was told to place thirty pigs, three groups of ten, in three separate sties and leave them for a fixed number of days. The state of the pigs at the end of it, each group representing respectively the Goths, the Romans and the Byzantine soldiers, would give an indication of the future.

When the appointed day came, most of the Gothic pigs were dead while the majority of the Byzantine porkers were hale and hearty. Most interesting of all, however, was the fate of the Roman pigs. Although half of them survived, all of them had lost their hair.[1]

It is a slightly ridiculous story – even the historian Procopius in whose history we read the account, writes that he did not believe it – but it is as fair a reflection as any of the state of Italy at the end of the Gothic regime. The reign of Theoderic is one of the final flowerings of the country until the Renaissance; it was a 'golden age' writes one of the king's contemporaries,[2] and one about which we have a wealth of literary and archaeological material. He was a patron of the arts and an enthusiastic rebuilder of the Roman heritage. But he was not an emperor. What surprises about Theoderic's rule is how India-paper-thin that civilisation was and how rapidly it disintegrated after his death. In many ways, Theoderic's greatest success was to get history to believe the hype.

There is no doubt that under this young Goth, still in his early 40s, Italy began to recover from the ravages of war, the decline and general depression to which it had been exposed for so many years. Contemporary writers, even Byzantine ones, were generally positive. With barely restrained relief, one chronicle sums up his years in power: 'Theoderic was a man of great distinction and of goodwill towards all men. He ruled for thirty-three years. In his times, for thirty years, Italy enjoyed such good fortune that his successors also inherited peace.'[3]

Not since the times of the great Roman emperors Augustus and Trajan had Italy enjoyed such a resurgence, or at least so it appeared to those who lived through it. The language used has the familiar tones of politics, or rather that of modern speech-writers and spin doctors. Writings contain images of renewal, restoration and youthfulness. Cassiodorus, head of the civil service, it has been pointed out, was one of the first authors to use the adjective *modernus*, meaning modern or forward-looking, in a political context.[4]

Not a vast amount is known of Theoderic's childhood. He was born in roughly 452 (it is still a subject of debate and could have been a year either side), around the time of Attila's death. His father was an Ostrogothic commander called Theodemer, his mother a Gothic convert to Catholicism called Erelieva, though she took the name Eusebia after she had been baptised.

It has been argued, and with some justification, that it was a childhood in Byzantium that shaped Theoderic. By all accounts he was a good-looking child and from the age of 8, throughout most of the 460s, he lived in the Great Palace. He was a hostage to Emperor Leo I for Ostrogothic good behaviour, a condition of the peace that the Goths had agreed to following the dismemberment of Illyria. He spent these crucial years of development in the

Eastern capital receiving an imperial education. One contemporary historian suggests that he was illiterate, that he had been unable to learn to sign even the first four letters of his name; instead, Theoderic used a golden plate with the Latin word *legi*, 'I have read it', punched through. He would then stencil his name onto documents. Given his upbringing, stories of his illiteracy are either a mistake (the stencil was some kind of a seal) or simply fiction.[5]

There is little doubt that Theoderic gained from his early exposure to the empire. From the time of the Emperor Augustus and his elite school for foreign princes on the Palatine Hill in Rome, the sons of kings were often taught the tools of their craft alongside the empire's heirs. This education and the experience of international *Machtpolitik* was supposed to benefit both Theoderic and the Roman Empire; having got to know each other, it should have been apparent that the benefits of working together far outweighed any possible disadvantage.

And when Theoderic left court in around 470, the emperor went out of his way to keep the Ostrogoths on side. As he went to rejoin his father, now king, in Pannonia, Emperor Leo ensured that the young man took 'great gifts' with him.[6] At any rate, the next few years were the making of Theoderic. He proved himself as a commander and, on the death of his father, was appointed his successor.

As complex as the chronology is of the next few years in Italy, the silence of contemporary historians makes it more so for Gothic history, though what is clear is Theoderic's rapid rise and consolidation of his power in the Balkans. When Emperor Zeno was briefly usurped in 475, Theoderic helped him get back his throne. For the next few years he managed at times both to support Byzantium and to oppose it, such as when he plundered imperial lands in Illyria, but by the early 480s he was once more on side. And by 484 he was king of the Goths, racking up a significant number of honours. He had been appointed consul, commander-in-chief and given the honorary name Flavius. His role in helping Zeno regain his throne was recognised with a triumph through the streets of the capital and with an equestrian statue in front of the palace. But despite attempts to tie him more closely to the Byzantine cause, he remained his own man. A few years later he was again a freelance agent. In 486 he attacked Thrace and the following year snapped at Byzantium's heels, going so far as to cut off some of the city's water supply. Given what was not always the easiest relationship, it is not too surprising that Zeno positively encouraged Theoderic's invasion plans of Italy.

It is worth pausing to consider exactly what Theoderic had won once Odovacer had been murdered. After decades of civil war, Italy was in a disastrous state. Pope Gelasius gives an unpleasantly vivid impression of these years. His letters speak of famine, destruction, pestilence and war, and the widespread archaeological evidence of coin hoards supports the literary evidence of uncertainty. Despite the inevitable spin after the fact, it should not be presumed that Italy breathed a massive sigh of relief as soon as Theoderic had taken over. Sicily, for example, which Odovacer had managed to wrest back from the Vandals, remained distinctly suspicious of him. Even as partisan a writer as Cassiodorus comments on the 'hearts of provincials going astray' and their general 'mistrust' of Gothic rule. It was a period of intense confusion.[7]

This uncertainty was not helped, initially at least, because, as with Odovacer's rule, there was a question mark over Theoderic's status. Again a difference can be seen between the words used and actions taken. But either through force of character, or because Odovacer had set a precedent, this was resolved much more quickly. Theoderic might have been technically only king but in every regard he behaved like an emperor. Byzantium was deferred to with a nod rather than a bow, and other Western kings, rulers of 'foreign peoples', were his to order around. In a famous letter dated to the first decade of the sixth century in which he asks a patrician to find a lyre player to send to the upwardly mobile and ambitious Clovis, king of the Franks, Theoderic hopes that the musician's 'sweet sound' will tame 'the savage heart of the barbarian'.[8] It is hardly the tone of one equal to another.

These imperial pretensions and aspirations come together in the one confirmed representation of Theoderic that has survived, a medallion called the Senigallia medal, found at the end of the nineteenth century and now in the National Museum in Rome. The image of Theoderic himself on the medal is fascinating because it is so explicitly Roman. Everything, from the Beatles-style mop-top, which was de rigueur for late Roman rulers, and the staff he is carrying bearing the goddess Victory to his military armour and cloak, is absolutely Roman. For a barbarian to portray himself as such was not in itself out of the ordinary. What marks such a significant change is how imperial the representation is.

Most surprisingly of all, Theoderic is wearing Romulus Augustulus' ornaments, the ones that Odovacer had sent, cap in hand, to Emperor Zeno. The current Eastern emperor Anastasius sent them to him by 493. There is no doubt that could one see the colour of the cloak on the medal it would have been purple, the colour of emperors and, according to legend, first worn by Rome's founder. In earlier times the wearing of the colour by anyone other than the emperor himself would have meant death, but a rather peevish letter survives from Theoderic chasing his imperial robes. 'If you have any care for your own safety, come at once with the purple,' he threatens the manufacturer. This was a step beyond anything that Odovacer had done. The not-so-subtle subtext of Theoderic's words to the Eastern emperor that 'our royalty is an imitation of yours', is not just that he was aping the East but that it was as legitimate.[9]

But, and it is a hugely significant qualification, there is something not quite right about the image. Rather like a child's spot-the-difference puzzle, you have to stare at it for a moment or two before you realise what is wrong with Theoderic's face. And then it hits you. He is wearing a moustache. Although there are many statues, coins and pictures of Romans from every end of the empire wearing a beard, there is no image in the whole history of the empire showing a Roman wearing a moustache on its own. Indeed, as Bryan Ward-Perkins points out, there is not even a Latin word for 'moustache'.[10]

For all that, the social language that Theoderic used was entirely Roman. And even though there was no suggestion that he ever considered for a moment giving the system of government a more Gothic makeover, the moustache sounds an inappropriate discord. It points to a disharmony between the Roman and Goth that could never be resolved.

At the start of his reign, this was not apparent. A recurring theme in politics, society and arts was continuity, which reflects the Goth's desire to calm tensions and ensure stability. The best way to get locals to accept him as a sovereign was to make sure his rule was a flavour that they recognised. He may have been a Goth, but to all intents and purposes this was Roman rule, with Roman laws, Roman taxes and Roman bureaucracy.

To take the most glamorous example of all, although he ruled out of Ravenna Theoderic deliberately celebrated his *tricennalia*, his thirty-year jubilee, in Rome in AD 500 (it is not known what exactly it was the anniversary of, though the best answer seems to date to it from his successes after returning from Constantinople as a child).[11] There was a draw to the city that no true Roman could resist. Constantine the Great, for example, had also hosted two jubilees in the city, and he was an emperor who had relocated the capital.

The only contemporary image of Romulus Augustulus. A gold *solidus* of the emperor helmeted, cuirassed, with a spear over his right shoulder and a shield on left. *(The Bridgeman Art Library)*

The missorium of Theodosius in the Real Academia de Bellas Artes de San Fernando, Madrid. *(Giraudon/The Bridgeman Art Library)*

Diptych depicting Stilicho, his wife Serena and their son Eucharius in the basilica di San
Giovanni Battista, Monza, Italy. *(akg-images)*

Palatium mosaic in the basilica of Sant' Apollinare Nuovo showing the palace and the city of Ravenna. *(Ravenna Tourist Office)*

An ivory and metal cameo depicting Emperor Honorius and his wife, Maria. *(Giraudon/The Bridgeman Art Library)*

Above: A detail from a mosaic in the basilica of Sant' Apollinare Nuovo showing the harbour at Classis. *(Ravenna Tourist Office)*

Below: Fresco of a seaside villa from Stabiae, now in the Museo Archeologico Nazionale, Naples. *(The Bridgeman Art Library)*

A first-century fresco from Stabiae showing a view of the harbour of either Stabiae or Puteoli. *(akg-images/Erich Lessing)*

Lucullanum as it looks today. A view from the Via Partenope of the Castell dell' Ovo and the Borgo Marinaro. *(akg-images/Tristan Lafranchis)*

Eugène Delacroix's Attila destroying Italy and the Arts, in the library of the French National Assembly, the Chamber of Deputies in the Palais Bourbon in Paris. (*Giraudon/The Bridgeman Art Library*)

Above and right: The tomb of Theoderic the Great in Ravenna. *(Ravenna Tourist Office)*

Andrew Pleavin as Orestes in the 2001 film *Attila*. *(Andrew Pleavin)*

Thomas Sangster as Romulus Augustulus and Ben Kingsley as Ambrosinus in the 2007 film *The Last Legion*. *(Keith Hamshere)*

It must have been a glorious occasion, the likes of which a punch-drunk Rome had not seen for many years. Theoderic was met outside the city by both the senate and the pope, who then escorted the Goth across the River Tiber to a spot called the Golden Palm. This was the area between the Curia Senatus and the Arch of Septimius Severus where the emperor traditionally made public appearances. And it was here that Theoderic addressed the crowd.

For the pomp and circumstance of this event it is fortunate that we have an eyewitness: a 32-year-old North African bishop from what is now Tunisia. Fulgentius, the greatest North African theologian after Augustine and, as we shall see later, possibly the last writer to mention Romulus Augustulus when he was alive, happened to be visiting Rome at the time. He comments on the 'noble appearance of the Roman senate', the 'varied ranks of the aristocracy each with its own distinctive insignia', and the 'shouts and cheers of a free people'. But festivals like this left him cold – Rome could keep such events. His anonymous biographer goes on say that the bishop saw nothing worthwhile in this spectacle, nor was he attracted by the useless enjoyment of such worldly vanities.[12]

The cavils of a party-pooping prelate aside, the celebrations seem to have been a success. They were topped by games in the Circus Maximus, anachronistic perhaps, yet at some level expected, and when Theoderic himself appeared, the people of Rome whooped and cheered and called him a second Trajan or Valentinian. This was the behaviour of an emperor and his subjects.

What characterises Theoderic's rule above all was his ability to use the past to look forward. Rome's heritage was something to be nurtured, cherished and rebuilt. Theoderic wrote to the state architect in Rome: 'Past princes should rightly owe me their praise: I have conferred long-lasting youth on their buildings, ensuring that those clouded by old age and decay shall shine out in their original freshness.' He grasped the concept, just like the Emperor Augustus had done half a millennium before him (as indeed both Napoleon and Adolf Hitler via his architect Albert Speer were also to understand), that civic pride reflects glory both on its citizens and by default also on its rulers.[13]

As Theoderic had recognised with his celebrations in Rome, whatever the actual political status of Rome might have been, people still thought of it as the centre of Roman power. The restoration of the city, especially after the repeated sackings and neglect of the previous decades, was the way to win the hearts and minds of the people, and Theoderic appears to have made a particular effort in this direction. He restored the imperial residence on the Palatine Hill, repaired city walls and the senate building.

But Theoderic realised that a spring clean was not enough. He also looked at the infrastructure. The most visible sign was the restoration of the city's water supply. In Rome, the man in change of aqueducts was ordered to pull up 'hurtful' trees that were undermining foundations and to repair the masonry, making that the priority. Faced with an empty exchequer, fifty years earlier Valentinian III had ordered the city to make do as best as it could on its own. The state was now taking charge again. Aqueducts and sewers were spruced up and granaries were repaired.[14]

More than simply encouraging rebuilding work, there is an indication that Theoderic backed this up with a tough stance on crime. He put a halt to those who customarily helped themselves to lead off the roofs and brass decoration from public buildings. When commissioning much of the restoration work, he warns that this is not a licence for fraud. 'Let there be no corrupt practices in reference to the distribution of the water,' he cautions, an indication of how little town councils have changed. His attention to detail was such that on hearing that a bronze statue had been stolen in Como, he offered a free pardon and 100 gold pieces to anyone who was prepared to turn the culprit in. And if no names were put forward, then all the city's workmen were to be called together and tortured until the culprit confessed. 'Such a piece of work as moving this statue can only have been undertaken by some craftsman,' he explains.[15]

Measures like these had an impact on health and the general quality of living. It was an early example of what modern sociologists call the broken windows theory. The idea that if problems – be they broken windows or run-down aqueducts – are fixed and maintained when the problems are small, then society improves. In modern times it was a concept used to great success in cleaning up New York in the 1990s under then mayor Rudolf Giuliani. This is precisely what Theoderic was trying to do – give people back quality of life and pride in community, all of which then reflected back on him.

Confirmation that his restoration work had a higher purpose is seen in his specific concern for the Theatre of Pompey. This had been the very first stone theatre built in Rome and was one of the city's showpieces. Remains of it can be seen in Largo di Torre Argentina and off the Via di Grotta Pinta underground to this day. Theoderic was not just concerned with practical matters: as he himself said, he decided to have it repaired, so that 'what was bestowed on Rome for the glory of the country, will not disintegrate under its descendants'.[16]

I have focused here on Rome, but this should not give the impression that the rest of the country was neglected. A vivid picture emerges in the letters of Cassiodorus of new cities being founded throughout Italy, city walls that had suffered in the wars being repaired and collapsed buildings being rebuilt. Pavia and Verona, the second and third cities of Theoderic's kingdom, were also adorned with palaces, baths, amphitheatres, and city walls.

The greatest effort by far was put into Ravenna, the royal capital, an administrative town full of Gothic bureaucrats – Canberra to Rome's Sydney. First of all it too was spruced up. As in Rome, water supply problems were exacerbated by the city's unsympathetic topography, and the broader population was dragooned into taking responsibility, renovating the aqueduct that had originally been built by Trajan and so on. A great deal of building took place, predominantly in the eastern part of the city. There is the Arian church complex – the toad-like church of San Spirito with its baptistery still stands, though the bishop's palace no longer exists – as well as several other churches both inside the city walls and just outside.

Without a doubt, however, the most impressive building was Theoderic's own palace. All too little is known about the official residence the Goth built there or rather the second-century structure he remodelled along the lines of the imperial palace in Constantinople (it should not be confused with the Palace of the Exarchs, which is later). The few contemporary references, however, are impressive. It was beautifully decorated with marble, gold, gems and mosaics, and surrounded by a portico. Archaeological evidence is sadly much too thin (it was partially excavated in 1908–14), partly because of later building on the site and partly because Charlemagne removed most of the interior decorations at the same time as he removed the statue to Zeno that Odovacer had erected.

The glory of Theoderic's Ravenna can be seen in the Palatium mosaic in the church of San Apollinare Nuovo. In the mosaic you can still see a marvellous building, triple-arcaded porch, flanked by two wings of porticos. An inscription above it, 'Palatium', both describes it as the palace and gives the mosaic its name. Another inscription, 'Civitas Ravenn[a]', the city of Ravenna, shows the city itself. Although it is hardly a map, it is possible to identify some of the structures, city gates and other churches. As diplomats shuttled back and forward between Ravenna and Constantinople they cannot have failed to notice Theoderic's growing aspirations.[17]

The renaissance was not just confined to the fields of architecture and civic rebuilding. The same idea can be seen quite clearly both in Theoderic's coinage and in the literature that flourished in his reign. Coins issued in Rome, for example, display the helmeted goddess Roma, a personification of the city, on one side, while the other bears the image of the city's founders, Romulus and Remus, suckling on the wolf. It is an echo of a Rome that most had thought long-forgotten. As one historian has noted, the closest parallel to the strength of this iconography is to be found in a series of bronze medallions issued under Constantine some two centuries previously. Theoderic himself recognised the statement that he was making. This was not just a measure to celebrate and advertise the present: for the Gothic king it was a chance to 'remind future generations of our times'.[18]

It is a similar story in literature, with what is generally dubbed the Ostrogothic revival. What characterises the language of all of those who wrote under Theoderic is a florid and deliberately classical style. His ministers Cassiodorus and Boethius are rightly regarded as the two last writers who can claim a place in the literary pantheon of ancient Rome, but the revival also includes less-well-known authors such as Rusticus Helpidius, Maximian the Etruscan and Ennodius. They may be difficult to understand and their pyrotechnically complex allusive style can be deeply frustrating to the modern reader, but what is important is that they were part of this rebirth.

Within this environment of continuity and stability it is possible to detect an economic boom. It was this that helped pay for the extensive costs of the building programme. Economics was clearly a field of interest to the king, and the *Anonymous*

Valesianus goes so far as to call Theoderic a 'lover of manufacturers', a view confirmed by the briefest of skims through the letters of Cassiodorus. One moment he is encouraging mining for gold in Calabria, or iron works in Dalmatia; another he is authorising the building of workshops near the forum in Rome; elsewhere he is passing legal protection for potters.[19]

The most obvious effect of this boom was that prices came down. In the previous chapter we saw that wheat had risen to 2⅔ pints for a gold piece in a besieged Ravenna. During Theoderic's reign we have one reference that a single gold piece bought you 960 pints of wheat (or 30 amphorae of wine) while 400 pints to the gold piece seems to have been the normal rate.[20] Price comparisons between ancient and modern times are both difficult and not necessarily useful. Purchasing power meant something different in late antiquity and it is certainly unfair to compare prices in a city under siege with one at peace; nonetheless, it gives a broad indication that prices were dropping.

Beyond the lower wheat price, evidence of the economic resurgence can be seen from the fact that Italy became not merely self-sufficient in grain production but was able to export and support other communities with its excess production. In around 510 Theoderic had sent grain supplies along with his army, so that the local land would not suffer through having to provide for the soldiers, a thoughtfulness that was then unheard of – though the more cynical have seen this as a reflection of remaining tensions between Goths and locals. And elsewhere, famine in Liguria and Venice was eased by subsidised wheat from Pavia and Tortona in the case of the former, Treviso and Trento for the latter. 'It is too outrageous that the farmer should starve while our barns are full,' writes Cassiodorus indignantly.[21]

The low cost and excess of grain point to a sense of security, both immediate and long-term security. Theoderic was creating a society that felt no threat of invasion, one in which it was worthwhile planting crops and where farmers felt they would be alive come harvest-time.

How was this stability achieved? Certainly Theoderic would have had little success without officials who had worked under previous regimes. Of the officials we know by name who worked in government between 476 and 553 some 80 per cent were Roman. Continuity was achieved through these men, and a stint under Odovacer seems to have done their careers no harm whatsoever; indeed it was a bonus in some cases. This is best seen in the career of Petrus Marcellinus Felix Liberius, though it is certainly also true for Cassiodorus' father who had been Odovacer's finance minister and was later to be Theoderic's civilian head of state in Italy.[22]

Born in around AD 465, Liberius would have been in his late 20s when Theoderic seized power. Little is known of his family background, though it is safe to assume that he came from landed gentry and there are hints that he was from Liguria. He achieved prominence at the end of the reign of Odovacer. It is not known exactly what role he had played under his regime, but we do know that he remained absolutely loyal until the bitter end. This constancy, the refusal to desert Odovacer, seems not to have counted against him. On the contrary, it appears to have played in his favour. Cassiodorus calls him a man of integrity, while Procopius calls him unusually upright and honourable.[23]

Theoderic rewarded such honesty and faithfulness with the title of praetorian prefect of Italy, effectively first minister. Liberius may seem young to have held so senior a position, but one reason suggests itself. Although he was clearly talented and from an appropriately well-known family, Liberius could have been the best that Theoderic was able to find. To the Italians, Odovacer was not necessarily an ideal ruler, but he had been a familiar constant, ruling for thirteen years, and we have already seen the initial mistrust of the Gothic rulers. Hand-in-hand, the two tasks that were demanded of Liberius were fraught with difficulty. He had to manage tax affairs, the will o' the wisp of chasing greater revenues without increasing rates. Second, he had to manage the 'barbarian question'.[24]

It is remarkable how well he achieved these two aims. The difficulty with tax affairs is that the upper classes had polished avoidance to a fine art. It had become common practice at periodic intervals in the later empire to wipe the slate of all unpaid taxes. In theory this was a windfall for all. In practice, it only ever benefited the rich, who typically postponed payment until the next round of write-offs. Admittedly several years afterwards, Cassiodorus writes: 'I realised that the revenues were increased; you knew nothing of extra taxes.' Reading between the lines, the implication is that Liberius got the system working properly. It should not be underestimated how much of a boon this would have been to the exchequer. When the Emperor Julian carried out a similar crackdown on avoidance in the 350s, he was able to reduce tax bills by more than two-thirds.[25]

More awkward, though no less successful, was the implementation of settlement on Italian soil similar to the one that had triggered the uprising against Orestes and the forced abdication of Romulus Augustulus in the first place. It was a much more serious matter this time, since land does seem to have changed hands. Clearly there were many more people involved than there had been under Odovacer's uprising. This could well have been a poisoned chalice for the young career bureaucrat, but it was one of the high achievements of Liberius' career that he managed it, so much so in fact that it is mentioned on his epitaph. Contemporaries claimed that he 'united both the estates and the hearts of the Goths and Romans', and however much of an exaggeration that might have been, it reflects well on his diplomatic talents.[26]

It must have been with some sense of relief that Liberius' term of office ended when Theoderic visited Rome in 500. For the next ten years, Liberius seems to have gone into semi-retirement in Ravenna, though not remotely out of the private eye. He corresponded vigorously with Ennodius and watched as his son became consul. Still only in his mid-40s at the end of the decade, he was named first minister of Gaul by Theoderic. His career stretched on well into the sixth century, as he gained greater and greater glory as an international statesman. He was not to die until around AD 554, at the age of 89, and was buried in Rimini.

While Liberius' career is fascinating for the light it sheds on a Roman professional under the Goths, his significance for us is in his connection to Romulus Augustulus. Almost the last trace that we have of the former emperor is a brief letter written to him by Cassiodorus on behalf of Theoderic.[27] Dating to sometime between 507 and 511, it confirms certain property rights that Liberius had conferred on him and his mother in the Goth's early reign. The letter is headed simply: 'King Theoderic to Romulus'. The lack of title or honorifics is a possible reflection of the confusion and embarrassment that the former emperor's continued existence caused. Other former emperors had done the decent thing and either died or had themselves murdered. There was no precedent for quiet longevity.

It is appropriate that Our generosity hold firm and constant: since the wish of the Prince ought to be unshaken (because it is recognised to be firm by our order), it should not be subverted by the tricks of malicious men. We have decided, therefore, that any written grant which can be proved to have been given to you or your mother by the Patrician Liberius, according to Our commands, will remain in force and you should not be concerned that it will be questioned.[28]

What does it mean? What caused the note to Romulus, now a middle-aged man in his 40s? The letter refers to a grant that had been given by Liberius to Romulus, early in Theoderic's reign. In Liberius' capacity as financier, the pension of 6,000 gold pieces granted to the former emperor by Odovacer had come under his purview, and the note suggests that the Scirian's original annuity had been upheld.

It is plausible that the letter dates from the death of his mother. When Romulus was born, in roughly 463, it is likely that Barbaria was then in her mid- to late 20s. The timeframe of the letter above would put her in her 70s, a long but not unreasonable lifespan in the period. As we have seen, Liberius was 89 when he died; Cassiodorus lived until he was 93. Certainly a change in Romulus' personal circumstances like this would cause a reassessment of his privileges. It is to Theoderic's credit that he upheld Odovacer's original decision.

There is just possibly one more piece of contemporary evidence for Romulus Augustulus. The bishop of Ruspe, Fulgentius, who had witnessed Theoderic's celebrations in 500, wrote a letter to a former patrician called Flavius Theodorus in around 528. The politician had had a rather chequered career. Although he had achieved all the state's top positions, he and his brother had been accused of being political troublemakers in 509. In 525 he was still important enough to be included in a diplomatic mission to Constantinople that was led by Pope John I. Theodorus, with all the participants, was arrested on his return, though he alone seems eventually to have been released. This appears to have ended his career and, perhaps for reasons of political prudency, Theodorus devoted the rest of his life to religion.

Fulgentius' letter to the former diplomat and consul is full of encouragement for his new devotion to the ascetic life, but warns against the dangerous attractions of fame and prestige. In it the

North African bishop mentions in passing the 'lovely letter of the holy brother Romulus'.[29] Sadly there is no context given other than his name.

It is not unreasonable to think that Romulus would still have been alive at this time. He would have been in his mid- to late 60s. There is also nothing inherently wrong with the idea that Romulus and Fulgentius might have corresponded directly. Lucullanum was one of the literary centres of Christian Europe at the time and, given their shared interest in the writings of St Augustine, it is not too surprising to learn that the North African was a correspondent of Eugippius.

Of course, the phrase is too vague to carry much weight, but it is just possible that Romulus managed to outlast everyone, seven emperors and kings: Zeno, Anastasius and Justin in the East, Glycerius, Julius Nepos, Odovacer and even Theoderic in the West. The image of him, an old man in a library in Campania, corresponding with leading intellectuals of the day, his early life and elevation to power becoming an increasingly indistinct memory, is as attractive a thought as the beautiful boy in his teens.

If this has been a distraction from the reign of Theoderic, it is because a shift occurred in the final three years of Theoderic's life, from around 523 onwards. The end was marked by cruelty, confusion and religious conflict. It was almost as if Italy were being ruled by a different man.

There are of course any number of possible reasons. Theoderic was now elderly, in his 70s. With no son to succeed him, he was naturally concerned about succession to the throne. Then there were setbacks in his foreign policy. Africa had been a supposed ally for some time (though noticeable in its absence when Theoderic really needed it), but with the accession of a new king in 523, it became obvious that Africa would ally itself with Byzantium.

The most apparent area where Theoderic seemed to change was religion. In what was, for most of late antiquity, a real battleground, Theoderic had championed a multicultural approach. Although he himself was an Arian, he did not harass Catholics. Indeed, he appears to have been tolerant of all. So much so, in fact, that when Christians burned down a synagogue in Genoa he wrote what has become a much quoted statement of tolerance: 'I cannot command your faith, for no one is forced to believe against his will.'[30]

This multi-faith approach now changed. The *Anonymous Valesianus* is suitably hyperbolic on the subject. 'The devil found an opportunity to steal for his own a man who was ruling the state well and without complaint,' it says.[31] To this must be added, inevitably, all the portents of doom that normally accompanied a ruler losing his grip: a woman giving birth to snakes, the sudden appearance of comets and numerous earthquakes. All these are indications of the unhappy state in which Italy now found herself, though they were, of course, written after the event and are as much preparing the reader for Theoderic's death as a reflection on what was happening at the time.

Intolerance came to the fore with the death of Pope John on 17 or 18 May 526. John had unwillingly led the diplomatic mission to Constantinople mentioned above. He had been sent to ask Emperor Justin to stop the persecutions of Arians in the East. Although moderately successful, on his return all the diplomats involved were thrown into prison in Ravenna. John himself died a few days later. Although it seems to have been of natural causes, he was soon regarded as a martyr, and in accounts of the pope's life, Theoderic is referred to, for the first time, as 'the heretical king'.[32]

The perception of Theoderic as increasingly intolerant towards religion is merely the tip of the iceberg. It reflects the fracturing of the relationship between Goth and Roman. Cassiodorus might have written about Roman and Goth living together in perfect harmony, and many have taken his comments on the subject at face value. But multiculturalism was as sensitive an issue then as it is now. The reality appears to have been different. It is worth emphasising the huge disparity in the populations: Romans outnumbered Goths roughly forty to one. It is has been estimated that there were approximately 4 million Romans to 100,000 Goths.[33]

Old habits died hard, and assimilation occurred only at the most superficial level throughout the West. When Sidonius Apollinaris wrote to a friend saying: 'You avoid barbarians because of their bad name; I give them a wide berth even when they have a good one', he was painting a much more accurate picture. In matters of law, for example, Roman and Goth were judged differently. From Britain's own colonial history it is easy to comprehend how soon a two-tiered society could lead to resentment. How shallow the tolerance between the two parties was can be seen as early as 535, only nine years after Theoderic's death, when the senate declined to meet his successor in Ravenna. And at the end of Gothic rule, the majority of Romans in Italy supported the Byzantine invasion.[34]

Other than the legal split between Goth and Roman, although there are a few exceptions, for the most part the Goths concerned themselves with the military, the Romans with civilian matters. 'The Gothic army wages war so that the Roman may live in peace,' writes Cassiodorus. And this split was underlined by the physical divide between the two. This can be seen clearly in the pattern of Gothic settlement in Italy. While there were of course garrisons around Naples, south of Rome and protecting the Alpine passes, most Goths seem to have settled broadly in the north – quite clearly a reflection of military priorities.[35]

There is also the question of how much assimilation could really have occurred. A law of the Theodosian Code dating to the previous century is absolute on matters of marriage: 'No provincial of whatever rank or class he may be, shall marry a barbarian wife, nor shall a provincial woman be united with any foreigner. If there should be any alliances between provincials and foreigners through such marriages and if anything should be disclosed as suspect or criminal among them, it shall be expiated by capital punishment.'[36] There had always been a tradition of intermarriage at the highest level – Ricimer, as we have seen, married the emperor's daughter – but outside quite clearly political couplings, there is little evidence.

Although unions must have taken place in individual cases, it is also crucial to remember that they all seem to have been one way, Gothic men marrying Roman women. One of Theoderic's bodyguards, for example, married a Roman woman in Spain. And there are no examples of Romans taking a Gothic name. Theoderic's much quoted comment that 'a poor Roman plays the Goth, a rich Goth the Roman', is only half right. The second half was certainly true, but the first half was a little optimistic.[37]

The most significant sign of growing unhappiness between Roman and Goth was the trial and subsequent execution of the statesman Albinus and the philosopher Boethius, the latter the last writer who can claim a place in the literature of ancient Rome. While less significant at the time than the death of Pope John, certainly not as widely commented on, it is important for us not just because of the position that Boethius holds in the Western European literary canon but because of what it says about decaying Gothic/Roman relations.

Cyprian, Theoderic's public prosecutor (the Latin word is *referendarius*) accused Albinus of writing a letter to the Eastern emperor, Justin, which was hostile to the current regime. This was a treasonable offence. But what gave the case such an edge, what rocked Italian society, was that Albinus was a senior establishment figure. He was from one of Italy's leading families and had been Theoderic's first consular nominee.

The case was not entirely a fabrication. There is at least circumstantial evidence to damn Albinus, and it is likely at the very least that he had been in contact with Byzantium. His accuser had himself led a diplomatic mission to Constantinople which, as John Moorhead, who has analysed the case in some detail, observes, would have placed him in a good position 'to obtain damaging material or at least plausibly claim he had encountered such material'.[38] But if the charges were not entirely beyond the realms of possibility, the background to the affair was much more complicated and was rooted, behind the scenes, in political jealousy.

The accusation of Albinus in Verona was dramatic in the extreme. He of course denied all charges. The consul, senator and philosopher Boethius spoke in his defence. 'The charge of Cyprian is false, but if Albinus did that, so too have I and the whole senate with one accord done it. It is false, my Lord King,' he said.[39] Lacking material evidence, the prosecutor turned on the accused and his counsel, and they were both imprisoned.

Boethius' own account of the affair, naturally enough, is as partisan as Cyprian's accusations. He wrote his masterpiece, *Consolation of Philosophy*, in which he debates his fate with Lady Philosophy from his prison cell. It is a book that greatly influenced Western thought, was read by Chaucer and Dante and is arguably the last classical work of literature. But it also allows a greater insight into what occurred.

The crucial evidence against them was forged letters probably connected in some way with the charge against Albinus of having communicated with the East. Boethius himself is unequivocal that he was framed. 'As for the forged letters cited in evidence that I had hoped for the freedom of Rome, there is little purpose in speaking of them. It should have been obvious that they were forgeries had I been allowed to make use of what carries the greatest weight in all such matters – the confession of the very informers,' he writes.[40]

The charge against him was a serious one. It was the equivalent of treason and fomenting revolution. The phrase he uses, 'the freedom of Rome', is, as Moorhead points out, probably a euphemism for Byzantine intervention in Italy.[41] There are enough other uses of the word 'freedom' both in official correspondence and even in legislation to suggest that this is what its general political use was. It was enough to damn him.

Both he and Albinus were immediately imprisoned. History loses sight of Albinus, though there is no question that he was executed. Boethius was tried by a kangaroo court and executed near Pavia in the summer of 526. With lip-smacking relish we can read how he was tortured for a long time with a cord that was bound round his forehead so tightly, that his eyes cracked in their sockets. Then finally he was clubbed to death.[42]

A short time later, even a few days, Theoderic himself was to die, on 30 August 526. One rumour had it that it was of remorse. Spooked at the face of a fish which reminded him of a cabinet minister he had had executed, he took to his bed and, writes Procopius, hid under the blankets.[43] Psychological trauma aside, the physical symptoms appear to have been a repeated series of attacks of diarrhoea. He died three days later.

The mausoleum of Theoderic, which he had built just outside Ravenna, to the north-east of the city, is unique both in design and material. The limestone for the tomb had to be transported from the other side of the Adriatic Sea and stands in contrast to other – brick – buildings of the period. It is a fascinating structure to pore over to this day, and one of the highlights of a trip to the city. It is, as the art historian Edward Hutton so memorably comments: 'the only monument that remains to us of those confused and half barbaric centuries which lie between antiquity and the Middle Ages'. Even here Theoderic is seen aping Roman rather than Gothic heritage. The two-storey structure and the stone masonry hark back to the mausoleum of Diocletian in Split.[44]

Unfinished at the time of his death, it has a decahedron-shaped floor plan over two storeys, the upper, which originally held the tomb, slightly smaller than the lower. The ornamentation is simple and refers back to classical and early Christian roots, though there is little consensus on the iconography of the tomb. But it is the ceiling that takes your breath away: it is a single stone, almost 11 metres in diameter and weighing around 230 tonnes. As a feat of engineering it is incredible, though like Theoderic's reign it was flawed: it is split by an enormous crack.

And as for Ravenna, Romulus', Odovacer's and Theoderic's capital? It became a decaying memorial that the marshes tried to reclaim, 'lost in the fogs and the miasma of her shallow and undredged lagoons'. It was left the tomb of the empire.[45]

It is shocking how rapidly Theoderic's heritage was squandered after his death. The fate of Western Europe had lain in his hands, but it was crumpled up and tossed aside by his successors. By 535 General Belisarius of Byzantium had occupied Italy and by 536 the Ostrogoths had begun to fight among themselves. It took only another two decades for the remnants of Theoderic's rule to be consigned to the history books. Italy was left to enter the Middle Ages, led there by the Lombards.

If in the end Romulus was a child playing at being emperor, then, even more so than Odovacer, Theoderic was a small boy, dressed in a toga, pretending to be a Roman. Not only was little to remain of his heritage, his attempts at multiculturalism, for Goth and Roman to live side by side, soon vanished without trace too. As the Goths left Italy in 552, Procopius chillingly writes: 'they made it an incident of their progress to destroy without mercy the Romans who fell into their hands'.[46] The massacre of

300 child hostages from Campania was only the worst of their atrocities.

All too soon, the imperial insignia that Romulus Augustulus had proudly worn for his coronation in October 475 had left the West once more. The golden brooch hung with jewels, which had been given to Emperor Zeno then passed back to the West under Theoderic, was finally captured in Ravenna and taken back in Byzantium. Justinian is wearing it on his right shoulder in the famous mosaic in San Vitale in Ravenna. The last glimpse we have of it is at the accession of Emperor Justin II in 565. The imperial jewels were never again to return to the West.[47]

The British writer Patrick Leigh Fermor notes that after the murder of Boethius 'there was nothing but candles and plainsong left to lighten the shadows'.[48] Certainly the playful world of Ovid and Martial was left behind, and Western society had nothing to look forward to but the darkness of Beowulf.

FIVE

Imitation of Life

On the evening of 8 September 1941 British bombers released their explosive cargo over the town of Kassel in Germany. The target had been the city's armament factories and railway station, but the bombs also wiped out Kassel State Library, home to the *Hildebrandslied*, or *Lay of Hildebrand*. Little known in the English-speaking world beyond universities, it is the oldest extant heroic poem ever found on German soil. There is barely a German today who does not know the opening line by heart: '*Ik gihorta dat seggen . . .*'; I heard it told.

Written down by two scribes at some point in the 830s in the scriptorium of the monastery of Fulda, the manuscript formed the two outer leaves of a Latin biblical text called the Book of Wisdom, the *Liber Sapientiae*. It was total chance that it was written down at all. The cost of vellum was such that every inch of a parchment was typically covered. No one knows why it is that these two anonymous monks – they can be told apart by their handwriting; one is neat and tidy, the other more uptight and with erasures – decided to fill the space they had left with an epic poem. Crucially for this story the saga that survived those bombs from a later conflict is a snapshot of the struggle between Odovacer and Theoderic.

Outside the realm of academia, the importance of the classical world to the popular imagination and popular culture cannot be ignored: it reflects the manner in which historical characters become part of the fabric of our collective memories. The story of

133

Antony and Cleopatra is much better known from Shakespeare than from any classical source. Cleopatra's face is either that of a beautiful, if heavily mascara-ed Elizabeth Taylor or the one drawn by French cartoonist Albert Uderzo, much more so than the real (if one is being honest) rather dumpy profile that stares out of contemporary coinage. Thanks to the dominance of television and Hollywood, for better or worse, Brad Pitt is Achilles; Alexander the Great to most people now has the face of Colin Farrell while his mother, Olympia, is irrevocably Angelina Jolie; and Romulus Augustulus looks like Thomas Sangster. It is no surprise that thirty years on, Derek Jacobi still finds himself hailed in the supermarket as Caesar when doing the shopping, such is the hold of *I Claudius* on the popular imagination to this day.

Although the afterlife of the historical figures in *The Last Roman* is in some ways, *pace* Attila, much less convoluted than that of Cleopatra or the Emperor Augustus, they do have distinct stories to tell. Rather than examine each character through all its permutations, which would take a book on its own for Attila, this chapter will focus on a number of them in a variety of artistic genres and in different periods of history. Odovacer and Theoderic through the epic poem the *Hildebrandslied*; Attila through Delacroix's decorative cycle, the ceiling of the library of the French National Assembly, the Chamber of Deputies in the Palais Bourbon in Paris; and Romulus Augustulus himself through various reincarnations from poetry and novels to Friedrich Dürrenmatt's play *Romulus the Great* and Valerio Massimo Manfredi's novel *The Last Legion*.

ODOVACER AND THEODERIC

Although it had sat quietly on the shelves first of all at the monastery of Fulda and then at the Court Library at Kassel for almost a thousand years, the *Lay of Hildebrand* achieved international recognition at the hands of the Grimm brothers. It is thanks to these siblings, better known for their work with folk tales, that this strange poem was named and publicised in 1812.

But it survived the Second World War bombing, as it had survived suggestions that it be presented to Adolf Hitler in 1937. With incredible foresight, as soon as the war had started the library's director had moved the manuscript to the underground vault of the nearby state bank. It was again luck that saved the *Hildebrandslied* during another, more serious, bombing raid, this time on 22 October 1943. Only two months before it had been moved again, out of harm's way to a cellar in the resort town of Bad Wildungen. And there it vanished.

A great deal has been written about German and Russian looting during the Second World War. Barely a year goes by, even today, without a lengthy court case taking place over the original ownership of one or other Old Master. As I write this today, for example, in January 2006, more than sixty years after the end of the war, Austria has been ordered to return five paintings by Gustav Klimt to the heir of a Jewish family that fled the country during the Nazi era. Much less acknowledged are the vast number of instances of US looting during the war.

Rumours circulated that the manuscript had been stolen and smuggled into Russia. But in *Bibliophiles and Bibliothieves*, her thrilling account of the manuscript's wartime and postwar adventures, Opritsa Popa traces how the manuscript had been picked up (his own words) by Bud Berman in the spring of 1945. Before his demob, the US army lieutenant brought it to the US and sold it to the famous New York booksellers the Rosenbach Company for $1,000. Despite the clear stamp 'Ex bibliotheca Cassellana', from the library in Kassel, which was subsequently disfigured by the bookseller, the *Liber Sapientiae* with the second leaf of the *Hildebrandslied* was sold to an aged book collector in California. This sale went ahead despite an expert at the Pierpont Morgan Library recognising the manuscript and identifying it as such. In August 1953 it was eventually retrieved from the Doheny Memorial Library in California and returned to Kassel.

But the trail for the first leaf, which had clearly been carefully detached, had gone cold. It took another nineteen years for the Rosenbach Museum in Philadelphia – the museum that grew out of the holdings of the original booksellers – to admit that they had had it all along. And in September 1972 the two manuscripts were finally reunited.

The history that the poem depicts is fascinating, representing as it does both a distorted and telescoped impression of the three-year war between Odovacer and Theoderic at the end of the fifth century. In form, the epic is in the same mould as those like Beowulf; some sixty-eight lines of alliterating verse that had made the shift from oral composition to writing.[1] Not too successfully in fact, as it is a High German poem that someone has ineptly tried to put into Low German. There seems to be a section missing and it was inexpertly Christianised at some point.

In terms of characterisation, Theoderic is represented very much as the injured party, though he is an unconventional hero. He has not only been driven into exile by Odovacer's wrath, he has run away. And as everyone knows, heroes never run.

> ... My people –
> old and learned men, who lived long ago –
> said that my father's name was Hildebrand. Hadubrand is mine.
> He fled into exile from Odovacer's anger,
> went east with Theoderic and all his followers.

Theoderic had taken refuge at the court of Attila, lord of the Huns, who gave Hildebrand, son of Heribrand, a rich present:

> . . . a torque of wrought bullion,
> imperial gold, the gift of a great king,
> the Lord of the Huns.

The symbolism of the gift aside (as both metaphor and material it has generated a terrifying mountain of debate), the fact that the torque was made of 'imperial gold' should come as no surprise. Looked at purely historically in the context of the fifth century, Attila's power rested on his ability to reward those who supported him. The amount of tribute the Huns were claiming every year from 430 onwards was vast, and it is also worth remembering the massive tribute that Attila's uncle and then Attila himself had negotiated from Byzantium.

Now, after an exile of thirty years, Theoderic is returning to claim back his kingdom with Hildebrand by his side. If the epic is indeed the transcribed version of an earlier oral story that at some point in its history crossed the Alps, it is perhaps not too surprising that Odovacer is both the aggressor and the villain of the piece. As one eminent medievalist points out, Theoderic's coup and assassination of Odovacer 'was recast in the legend on the strength, presumably, of his later successes'.[2] History always did favour the victor.

The *Hildebrandslied* itself is a subversion of the common Freudian theme of the boy killing his father, seen elsewhere, for example, in the myth of the Irish hero Cuchullain. It is constructed around the idea that Hildebrand is facing a warrior called Hadubrand, otherwise unknown to him, in preparation for single combat, either as champions of Theoderic and Odovacer respectively or simply through cruel fate. Though in a twist to the myth, neither Hildebrand nor Hadubrand have any quarrel, indeed do not even know of each other's existence. It is simply the luck of battle that brings them to face each other.

Much effort has been wasted in trying to identify a historical prototype for Hildebrand. It is almost certain that he is imaginary. But what the reader knows and Hildebrand comes to realise is that the man facing him is the young son he abandoned when he went into exile with Theoderic and his army:

> He left behind, alone,
> a young bride and a baby not yet born,
> a child with no inheritance. Eastwards he went.
> Since then Theoderic would have been lost
> without my father, friendless exile that he is,
> bearing Odovacer only hatred.

Hadubrand refuses to believe that the man facing him could be his father. He knows that his father, just like anyone who could have identified him, is dead. Hadubrand is convinced that the man in front of him is trying to distract him with words and presents – the torque mentioned earlier. And anyway, a man of this age on a battlefield can only have survived by some underhand means. Although Hildebrand attempts to avoid the fight, combat is inevitable:

> 'Only the most cowardly of all the Huns,' said Hildebrand,
> 'would waver, now that you want so much
> to fight. So let us see
> which warrior must forfeit his weapons,
> and who shall carry off both mail coats.'

After a few lines describing the battle, the manuscript breaks off. It is not clear even if there was a third page to the manuscript, but there is no doubt about the outcome of the battle. Hildebrand manages to preserve his honour, but the cost is the death of his own son. The presumption is that Theoderic will then return to Italy victorious to take the crown.

In Western Europe, the folk memory of Theoderic was as strong as that of Attila. He became Dietrich of Bern (Theoderic of Verona) in a series of epics in the thirteenth century and puts in an important cameo appearance at the end of the *Nibelungenlied* as a Christian knight. Perhaps the most intriguing evidence of his widespread survival across Europe is the most famous and longest runic inscription, the Rök stone, which dates to the beginning of the ninth century. Discovered in an old church in 1840 in Sweden, the text is both convoluted and much debated, but it refers to 'Theoderic the bold' having been dead for nine generations.

ATTILA

Of all the characters from this period, it is Attila who needs no introduction. At the time of writing, a swift scan of the fiction section of any large bookshop offers readers the choice of Ross Laidlaw's and William Napier's novels, both called *Attila: The Scourge of God*, William Dietrich's *Scourge of God* or Michael Curtis Ford's *The Sword of Attila*. Those in the business section can pick up Wess Roberts's *Leadership Secrets of Attila the Hun*.

Although he is a hero in Hungary, where to this day Attila remains a popular boy's Christian name – Attila József was one of the foremost Hungarian poets of the twentieth century – both the traditional difficulty of the Magyar language and more recently the Iron Curtain has stopped that tradition travelling much beyond the country's boundaries. It means that for Western Europe he has long been a nightmare figure, the archetypal barbarian at the gate. The name of his tribe too, since the turn of the century, has become pejorative shorthand for Germany, more so than either Boche or Jerry. The term became fixed in the popular mind in Britain as 'the shameless Hun' (almost always singular) thanks to Rudyard Kipling. At the end of the First World

War, on the day before armistice, for example, the British newspaper *News of the World* carried the headline 'Hun surrender certain'.[3]

Attila has developed a mythic quality. In the Middle Ages he became the 'scourge of God', the *'flagellum dei'*, purifying the sins of the world with blood. He was certainly a concept in the Germanic sagas. As well as the *Hildebrandslied*, he appears in another epic called *Waltarius* and Germany's *Iliad*, the *Nibelungenlied*, though it is a little surprising that Richard Wagner decided to drop the character, by then called Etzel, from his Ring. Less threateningly, he appears in *The Pardoner's Tale* as a warning against drunkenness. Chaucer cautions that 'a capitayn [Attila] shoulde live in sobrenesse'.

As was so often the case for notables from the Roman world, Attila suffered the usual indignities of having his life turned into stage plays and operas from the seventeenth to nineteenth centuries. By far the best is Giuseppe Verdi's *Attila*. Inspired by an article he had read by France's arbiter of literary taste, Madame de Staël, which summarised one of the more popular German plays, the Italian composer used Attila to capture the popular mood for Italian unification. The opera was first performed in March 1846 and is revived on a fairly regular basis.

Eugène Delacroix's decorative cycle, the ceiling of the library of the French National Assembly, the Chamber of Deputies in the Palais Bourbon in Paris, was painted during the reign of Louis-Philippe, best known as the subject of the Daumier cartoon where he turns into a pear. The rule of the Orleanist monarch was marked by a revival of interest in monumental painting. Delacroix's image of Attila is fascinating partly because the virtual impossibility of access makes it less well known than it should be (these mural paintings have been seen rarely in the past forty years) and partly because it epitomises the European perception of both Attila specifically and barbarians in general.

Under the patronage of Adolphe Thiers, Louis-Philippe's minister of the interior, Delacroix was commissioned to paint on a grand and epic scale, public works in the manner of the old masters he admired. 'Small pictures get on my nerves, bore me, and big easel pictures done in the studio are as bad, they tire me out and I spoil them,' the artist wrote.[4]

In the spring of 1833 he was handed the Salon du Roi in the Palais Bourbon in Paris. It was a slightly surprising commission from Thiers. Delacroix had virtually no experience in large-scale work like this, certainly not for the king's reception room. It was a gamble for the future prime minister, too. Virtually all other decorations in the Palais Bourbon went to much-better-known artists, and had it not worked out, as one art historian writes: 'It could have caused Thiers . . . to lose face, if not office, with his political peers.'[5]

It is fortunate for us that Thiers did so. Delacroix had thrown off classicism and naturalism and had embraced romantic high baroque. So successful was his execution that it was followed up over the next few years by commissions for the library in the same Palais; the library of the Senate at the Palais du Luxembourg (between 1838 and 1847), the ceiling of the Galerie d'Apollon in the Louvre (between 1848 and 1850) and the Salon de la Paix in the Hôtel de Ville (1851 to 1855). All but the last survive – it was destroyed during the Paris Commune in 1871 – and as the art historian John Russell says, they: 'constitute a body of work which would be difficult to equal in any one city and by any one man, since the Renaissance'.[6]

The library is a cathedral-like space, long, high and narrow, some 42 metres long and 10 metres wide, on a north–south axis and entered by a door halfway down the western wall. It is a particularly complex surface on which to paint as the ceiling is neither flat nor vaulted in the common way. This presented an immense challenge as Delacroix could not draw on any previous precedents for technical help. The ceiling itself is divided into five cupolas in a row with a semicircular vault at either end. Lighting too presented a problem. Although the cupolas themselves are moderately well lit, courtesy of a series of windows on either side of the room, the semicircular vaults at both ends remain permanently in semi-darkness.

In terms of images, Delacroix assigned each of the cupolas a different theme. As he explained in a press release at the end of January 1848, the themes of Poetry, Theology, Law, History and Philosophy and Science, 'recall the categories adopted in all libraries without ever following the exact classification'. Other than the hemispheres at either end of the library, each of the cupolas is decorated by four appropriate scenes, classical or biblical in subject matter. In a note to himself he wrote: 'Ancient [themes] only – one can't have modern dress and ancient dress next to each other'.[7]

As you enter the library your eyes are first drawn to the cupola above. It is entirely appropriate for the setting, four scenes depicting Law: the well-known and eloquent lawyers Cicero and Demosthenes, Numa Pompilius, the first king of Rome, and the legendary Spartan legislator Lycurgus. Only then do you become aware of two half domes, one to your left, another to your right. Calm or violence, these are the choices that are presented to society. To one art historian Delacroix intended to show the 'fragility of civilisation',[8] its dawn and its twilight, though the obvious message from where you are standing is that Law is the fulcrum, the point that keeps society in balance while the themes of the five cupolas can only flourish in that state.

Thankfully rejecting his original intentions to balance the poet Petrarch at one end of the library with Socrates at the other, on the half dome on your left as you enter is *Orpheus Civilising the Greeks*, which was started in April 1843. Sitting in an idealised pastoral landscape with mountains and trees and surrounded by human figures and animals, Orpheus is not just the bringer of the arts, he is the father of mankind. The squatting creatures at his feet, most of them innocently naked, suggest that before his arrival, mankind was barely distinguished from the animals. But rather than the traditional lyre with which Orpheus is depicted, here it takes a second glance to realise that what he is holding is a scroll. Words and reading are powerful and appropriate symbols given the setting.

Delacroix himself jotted down some notes on his first pencil sketch of Orpheus, now in the Palais Bourbon Library. These are not just key to how he saw Orpheus, but also how he saw Attila, as it is the antithesis. 'In the first he has represented man in a state of nature, prey to all of the miseries brought about by all the necessities of life, invited by Orpheus to enjoy the benefits of the state of society – in the second, man now living in a state of civilisation, offers a sacrifice to Ceres and Bacchus.' These he had scribbled down from a periodical in January 1843.[9]

At the opposite end of the room is *Attila Destroying Italy and the Arts* which was begun towards the end of the same year. The contrast to Orpheus is immediate and shocking. Attila himself holds a spear in his left hand, a Morningstar in his right, and sits astride a white horse trampling over Eloquence and the Arts. The link with Orpheus is made explicit from the outset (the figure nearest the Hun king – the Arts – is holding both a lyre and a scroll) and the two images are tied together though it is significant that they cannot be viewed at the same time. This is a much more sophisticated representation than the cartoonish figure of destruction. Attila himself is centre stage, framed on our left by a broken Corinthian column and on the right by flames, smoke and burning. One of the figures, Eloquence, in the foreground is holding aloft a caduceus, the staff of Mercury. It is not just wanton destruction that is being portrayed, it is specifically the death of the ancient world.

Alongside the notes for Orpheus mentioned above, there is another note from the same periodical, a piece of reportage from a journalist who had toured Moscow and remembered Napoleon's invasion of Russia. Delacroix scribbled down: 'These old walls had trembled at his approach and the inhabitants of this town had fled before him as once the fields of Italy had been deserted by their inhabitants before Attila's horse – Attila tramples Italy and the arts.'[10] It is easy to see how the image of a burning city and fleeing inhabitants inspired the final piece. It has been suggested that this equation with Napoleon (Delacroix's admiration for the pugnacious Corsican is well known) is the reason that Attila appears aggressively undaunted.

It is artistically heretical to compare Delacroix with anything that Hollywood could produce. Certainly with an unrecognisable Jack Palance as Attila the Hun in the 1954, Douglas Sirk-directed *Sign of the Pagan*. The film is a rather campy Cinemascope production – the bass-intoned introduction speaks of 'a fierce plague of Mongol horsemen', led by the 'most ruthless conqueror of all time' – and suitably semi-dressed damsels exhibit as much décolletage as 1950s America would allow. The history might be negligible, but it does portray the same image of Attila as a force of nature.

Compare this then with the other well-known Old Master impression of Attila, which Delacroix certainly knew, if only from engravings. The fresco by Raphael, *Attila Repulsed from Rome by Leo I* in the state apartments of the Vatican, commissioned by Popes Julius II and Leo X at the beginning of the sixteenth century, is very different. Focusing on how Attila had been turned away from Lombardy (though here the story is set in Rome) Pope Leo (who has the face of his ninth eponymous successor) sitting on a white mule, is surrounded by cardinals and their retinue. Significantly, however, St Peter and St Paul, surrounded in brilliant white light and visible only to the Huns, put, quite literally, the fear of God into them.

Setting aside the political aspect to Raphael's painting (it is associated with the withdrawal of the French troops from Italy after 1512), and although there is a similar contrast between light and dark, sylvan peace and burning movement as in the Delacroix painting, Raphael's Attila looks somehow fearful, turning away in flight. It does not work quite as well.

In the end, Delacroix presents a depressing point of view. The veneer of civilisation that he depicts is painfully thin. Elsewhere in the library, Archimedes is randomly killed by a soldier; Pliny the Elder can do nothing to prevent the destruction of Pompeii by Vesuvius, Aristotle is pondering a skull and even the death of John the Baptist is one of the more fickle deaths in the Bible. Indeed, a large number of the characters presented suffered either great loss or violent death. It is apparent that there is little that mankind can do to prevent its destruction. It is unlikely that he had ever read Sidonius Apollinaris, but both the French painter and the bishop recognised and preserve this of all the Hun's characteristics, his elemental nature.

ROMULUS AUGUSTULUS

Artists have tended to work around Romulus Augustulus. It has always been easier and more potent to keep him as the symbol of the end, rather than try to flesh him out as a real person. The hunched dwarf-like Antonio Gramsci, leader of the Italian Communist Party in the 1920s, is best known today for the essays on fascism and capitalism he wrote in prison from November 1926 until his death in 1937. But in a paean to the Russian revolutionary Lenin, who had died in January 1924, he warned his readers off Benito Mussolini. Il Duce, a former friend and confidante when he was still a socialist and editor of the worker's paper *L'Avanti*, was now prime minister. Gramsci describes the dictator's 'eyes rolling in their sockets, the clenched fist ever raised in menace', and warns that while Rome has seen Romulus and Augustus in the past, it has also seen Romulus Augustulus.[11]

It was an emperor reduced to rhetorical device.

A similar approach can be seen in *Last Things*, a 1996 short story by Darrell Schweitzer. A slight piece, a detective story, the deposition of Romulus simply represents the loss of order. Odovacer is chaos. There is no attempt to characterise either leader: they are merely signifiers, crude shorthand for opposing ends of a society in decline.

Despite the lack of historical colour, the absence of artistic interest in Romulus is odd, precisely because the same period in the East has always attracted the attention of poets. Best known of all are W.B. Yeats's masterpieces 'Sailing to Byzantium' and 'Byzantium' and Charles Williams's 'Prelude'. The image of sensual decline, death-in-life, life-in-death seems to have struck a chord with poets in the English-speaking world.

Late antiquity in the West has inspired far fewer poets, but two twentieth-century poets in particular, on either side of the Second World War, shared a poetic interest in the decline and fall of the Roman Empire and saw in it a contemporary relevance: C.P. Cavafy and W.H. Auden.

Constantine Cavafy's exquisitely painful 'Waiting for the Barbarians', was first published in 1904. For the Alexandrian poet it was a significant work; in it he arguably found his mature voice. It is a dramatic dialogue between two observers trying, unsuccessfully, to come to grips with the world around them. To the repeatedly naive questions of the former as to why the city's people are behaving the way they are, the latter keeps answering: 'Because the barbarians are coming today.' It appears that Cavafy had no specific city or event in mind; indeed, the period itself is not even stated, though it is clear that the fifth century is intended, and it is easy to read the city as Rome.

What the poem does above all is to capture the paralysis and bewilderment at a civic level of the empire in the face of barbarian invasions. There is incomprehension as to how best to respond to them. The civic leaders of this unnamed city have got up early and put on their finery to meet them. The senators have stopped legislating, the emperor is there to greet them and to hand over a scroll 'loaded with titles, with imposing names'; the consuls have dressed up in their pomp to welcome them. It is only in the last epigrammatic couplet that an answer is given: 'those people are a kind of solution'. Such is the despair of the city that the barbarians are an answer. In the end they do not arrive and the citizens of the town are left worrying what the future might bring when even this solution does not appear.

Auden too was drawn to antiquity on several occasions, from 'Roman Wall Blues', one of his most anthologised poems, the song of a miserable soldier on Hadrian's Wall written in 1937 to his 1968 poem 'Rois Fainéants' where he satirises the impotent grandeur of the Merovingian kings. But the end of the Roman world kept drawing him back. 'An Encounter', imagines the meeting between Attila and Pope Leo, while his 1947 poem 'The Fall of Rome' is full of strange forebodings. 'Fantastic grow the evening gowns', as tax collectors chase defaulters through 'the sewers of provincial towns'. And he is writing as much about his own feelings on the matter as those of society. 'The Roman Empire is an historical phenomenon towards which no Westerner can feel either indifferent or impartial,' he says in his March 1966 essay 'The Fall of Rome'.[12]

Auden was struck by the symbolism of Romulus and wrote about him on several occasions. His 1959 poem 'Secondary Epic' captures his most significant thoughts on the emperor. In Book VIII of the *Aeneid*, Virgil pastiches the shield made for Achilles in the *Iliad* (itself the subject of a poem by Auden). The god Vulcan hammers out a shield for the poem's hero Aeneas with scenes that 'predict' the future history of Rome up to Augustus' victory over Mark Antony. Auden wittily imagines a Gothic poet criticising the Roman poet Virgil for misrepresenting the future of Rome on the shield.

There was a tendency among postwar British poets to denigrate Virgil. 'Virgil never consulted the Muse: he only borrowed Apollo's slide-rule,' snapped Robert Graves for example, and Auden was no exception.[13] He starts his poem 'No, Virgil, no' and continues with a wonderful pastiche of Virgil's overblown style in the fifth stanza ('Now Mainz appears and starry New Year's Eve/ As two-horned Rhine throws off the Latin yoke'). But most of all, the Gothic poet through whom Auden speaks mocks Virgil for missing 'so clear a proof of Providence' that the names of 'the Catholic boy/ whom the Arian Odovacer will depose' hark back both to Romulus and to Augustus.

Late antiquity has been an inspiration to more modern poets. British-born Peter Porter's 'The Last Hours of Cassiodorus', sees 'Our state days pinioned in official letters,/ The *Variae* of sound administration', and asks almost plaintively 'After me what further barbarisms?' And in 'The Last Roman Poet' by the Portuguese poet Paulo Teixeira the theme of imminent loss is continued. 'As everything degenerates and collapses around him', the unnamed poet longs for a single moment of 'adverbial quiet'.

By far the most significant is the poem entitled 'Romulus Augustulus' by Gerardo Deniz. The Mexican poet has interwoven both the moment of the fall as well as the historical tradition of the emperor. Romulus himself becomes frustrated at the lack of material about him that has survived. 'I effaced my footprints so well/ that they'll never know anything,' says the young emperor from 'the shadows in Campania'. He himself is aware how insignificant he is, that men are nothing more than rats and that 'all the stupidity in the world will be required/ to begin another era'.[14]

It is a shame that Friedrich Dürrenmatt is not better known among English-speaking audiences. His 1949 play *Romulus the Great* (*Romulus der Große*), which the Swiss playwright himself dubbed 'an unhistorical, historical comedy', is a savage and often very funny fantasy on the basic ideas behind the story of Romulus Augustulus. As he himself wrote in the programme for the play's première in Basle on 23 April: 'Romulus Augustulus was 16 when he became emperor, 17 when he abdicated and retired to Lucullus' villa in Campania. His pension was 6,000 gold pieces and his favourite hen is said to have been called Rome. That is what is known historically.'[15]

In fact the story of the chickens originated with Procopius' account of Honorius being told about the sack of Rome in 410. It is so ludicrous that this lapse is both forgivable and worth citing:

They say that the Emperor Honorius in Ravenna received the message from one of the eunuchs, evidently a keeper of the poultry, that Rome had perished. And he cried out and said, 'And yet it has just eaten from my hands!' For he had a very large cock, Rome by name; and the eunuch understanding his words said that it was the city of Rome which had perished at the hands of Alaric. The emperor with a sigh of relief answered quickly: 'My good fellow, I thought that my fowl Rome had perished.'[16]

Dürrenmatt wrote this most Shavian of plays to the background of what was happening around him. On one hand he was mourning the world that had been lost after the Second World War and wanting to skewer the militarism and heroism that had led Europe into conflict. An inspiration was what he saw as the ridiculous debate in Switzerland over whether German officers such as Claus von Stauffenberg, who had attempted to assassinate Adolf Hitler on 20 July 1944, had been traitors. More than that, however, the play was a consequence of Switzerland's increasingly isolationist stance towards the end of the 1940s. This was a reaction to fears of East–West conflict as the Cold War geared up and to the growing recognition within the country of Swiss complicity with the Nazi regime. As Dürrenmatt himself wrote: 'I do not lament the state, the law, rather a state that is unjust . . . It is not a play against the state, but perhaps one against the super state'.[17]

The many layers of irony in the play are apparent from the beginning: the inversion of Romulus's nickname – from 'little Augustus', he is now 'the great'; that the play opens in the same way as virtually every classical tragedy, with the arrival of an exhausted messenger; that the structure of the play itself, apparently about the destruction of the classical world, is a pastiche of one of Aristophanes' comedies; and that the action takes place in 476 around the Ides of March, a date associated with the murder of Julius Caesar and the death of the Roman Republic. The last connection is emphasised during a botched assassination attempt when Romulus cries: 'Et tu cook'. In every manner possible Dürrenmatt tweaks our preconceptions about the Roman Empire.

The conceit of the play is that Romulus Augustulus is now an old man of about 50, a clown, married to an ambitious social climber (she describes herself as a descendant of Julian the Apostate, 'the last great emperor', missing of course the point that within a thoroughly Christian empire this was distinctly non-U) and with a grown-up daughter. Although emperor, he spends his days pottering around his country estate in Campania, its walls lined with busts of Roman historical figures, tending his chickens, all of which are named after Roman emperors.

Romulus: Augustus hasn't laid?
Pyramus: Nothing, Emperor.

Romulus:	Tiberius?
Pyramus:	None of the Julians.
Romulus:	The Flavians?
Pyramus:	Domitian. But from those, your majesty wishes to eat none.
Romulus:	Domitian was a dreadful emperor. He can lay as many eggs as he wants, I won't eat them.

Yet Romulus is the one real character in the play. When news breaks that Odovacer's army has made it as far as Pavia, the emperor continues to do what he has done for the past twenty years, calmly eating his breakfast and rearing his chickens. Romulus breaks the last gold leaf off his crown to pay the valets and the cook.

All the characters are caricatures, from his minister of defence Mares who claims that the military position is turning in Rome's favour ('it is improving from defeat to defeat' or 'the better the general the fewer troops he needs') and the bumbling minister of state Tullius Rotundus to the businessman Rupf with his vulgar, cliché-ridden management speak (his name is taken from the verb *rüpfen*, meaning 'to fleece' or indeed also 'to pluck'). The Emperor Zeno too makes an appearance. Dürrenmatt has the emperor, a pompous coward who lives in the past, seek asylum in Italy during the revolt of Verina:

| Zeno: | We cannot afford the luxury of petty suspicions between our two empires. We must now save our culture? |
| Romulus: | How? Is culture something you can save? |

Yet when the news breaks that the German army is approaching Zeno asks when the next boat leaves for Alexandria. 'I intend to continue my unyielding struggle against German-ness [*Germanismus*] from Ethiopia,' he says. Romulus in many ways appears the holy fool. 'We are provincials over whose heads a world is growing that we cannot understand,' he says.

He rejects Rupf's offer to buy off the Germans in return for his daughter's hand in marriage, saying that he will not sacrifice Rea for a doomed empire. It becomes gradually apparent throughout the play that far from being the fool, Romulus has planned to dismember the Roman Empire all along. Part of the comedy is the audience's misunderstanding of Romulus' motivations. At the beginning of the performance Romulus is dressed in the costume of a clown, which he gradually removes during the play. Realisation slowly dawns on the audience that the emperor is sick of the empire's savage corruption and cannot wait to see the barbarians take Rome. In a powerful exchange his wife tells him she is leaving him:

Julia: I am going to Sicily because I love my fatherland.
Romulus: You don't have a fatherland. What you love is an abstract idea of state which gave you the chance to become empress through marriage.

Their argument concludes:

Julia: You are Rome's betrayer.
Romulus: No, I am Rome's judge.

As Romulus will not resist the barbarians, his daughter's fiancé Ämilian plots to assassinate the emperor. The scene, itself a pastiche of Shakespeare's assassination scene in *Julius Caesar*, is a farcical failure. Before the daggers can find their marks, a cry stops the conspirators in their tracks. When the shout goes up that the Germans are coming they all run away in terror. Romulus is the only one to keep his head. 'When the Germans arrive, let them come in,' he says calmly.

When Odovacer finally appears in the fourth act he is not the savage barbarian that had been feared. He appears in civvies, is a chicken fancier too, loves Rome and describes himself as a farmer who hates war. The only distinguishing mark that he is a barbarian is that he is wearing trousers rather than a tunic.

Now one of the final twists. Rather than replace him, he wishes Romulus to keep the throne. If Romulus is nervous of the past, Odovacer is scared of the future. He is dreading the arrival of the power-hungry Theoderic (Dürrenmatt makes him Odovacer's nephew). Although seen only briefly on-stage as a polite and obedient young man, his presence is an inhuman Nazi caricature ('He dreams of world domination and the people dream with him') of whom Odovacer sighs: 'Some say he will be called Theoderic the Great, if I know those historians.' If Romulus remains emperor, then the world will be saved from a bloody and transient German empire.

In the end both leaders are cheated. Romulus is denied the self-sacrifice that would have made surrendering the empire worthwhile. At the same time he suffers the loss of his wife, daughter and cabinet, all of whom drown trying to escape to Sicily. Only Zeno manages to survive, making it to Alexandria and preserving the Eastern empire. Although the audience has begun to warm to this humorous, courageous pacifist, it is with a shock that it realises that however much he might disagree, Romulus is a true heir to Augustus, as much of an imperial monster as those like Domitian he so despises. Romulus has sacrificed his entire family and cabinet for an ideal.

Odovacer, too, is robbed of the political manoeuvring that would keep power out of the hands of his nephew when Romulus abdicates into what for him is the worst of all possible fates, retirement. The play's final irony is that it is only Odovacer who recognises Romulus' greatness. Everyone, including the audience, has been duped. In the drama's closing moments Odovacer says to the barbarian horde that has turned up: 'I never saw a greater man, and you'll never see a greater one either.'

In recent years there has been a brief flurry of fictional interpretations of Romulus. Alongside the short story *Last Things* mentioned above, two novels are worth acknowledging. First is *The Twelfth Vulture of Romulus* by Boris Raymond, which takes its title from the legend that Rome had been founded after Romulus had seen twelve vultures fly over the Aventine Hill to his brother Remus' six, and the belief, as a result, that Rome would last twelve centuries.[18] Writing through an elderly Cassiodorus, who has gathered together his notes to try to understand the fall of the empire, it looks back at the fifth century.

While the 2003 novel is undoubtedly flawed (there are a number of anachronisms and typographical errors), it has some charm. The events leading up to Odovacer's revolt are framed by the rise and fall of Orestes. Freed by the lack of hard historical evidence, Raymond is able to create ingenious motivations for his characters' behaviour. One of the drivers for Orestes' actions is given by a secret society called the Phoenix Circle, a group founded by Cassiodorus' grandfather, to preserve Rome and to resist encroaching barbarian power in the empire, while his solution for St Severinus' reluctance to reveal his origins (he is an escaped catamite) is entertaining and no more implausible than recent academic suggestions that he was a Roman consul.[19] Most successful of all is the focus on the relationship between Orestes and Odovacer. Their closeness in age gives Raymond the opportunity to portray them as adopted brothers. The dynamic between the Roman and the barbarian who can never be fully accepted gives the book a tension and personalises the fall of the empire.

Best known, however, is Valerio Massimo Manfredi's 2002 novel *L'ultima legione*, released in English in 2003 as *The Last Legion*. The novel begins with Romulus already enthroned in

Ravenna. Odovacer's troops have attacked Pavia and Orestes has escaped to Placentia which, in the novel, is his home. In the opening chapter what must have been widespread frustration and disillusionment within the military is captured. 'A new emperor practically every year, barbarians controlling all the main posts, and now, to top it all off: a snotty-nosed kid on the throne of the Caesars! A 13-year-old brat who hasn't even got the strength to hold up the sceptre is supposed to be running the world – the West at least,' says one legionary.

Orestes, the ideal father, is murdered still believing that he can negotiate with Odovacer ('They [the barbarians] have no interest in bringing about the fall of an empire that gives them land and money,' he says) and Romulus is captured by the Scirian. After the revolt, Manfredi provides a plausible reason for Odovacer to pension off Romulus. If he were to kill the emperor, says the boy's tutor, then Byzantium would never recognise Odovacer's authority. 'Even the great Ricimer, your predecessor, was forced to hide behind insubstantial imperial figures,' he says.

Inevitably in an adventure story, the action departs from historical fact. Romulus is exiled on Capri rather than to Lucullanum, allowing for an Errol Flynn-style escape from the island. The novel's true hero, Aurelius, one of the defenders of Aquileia against Attila, takes the remnants of the fictitious Nova Invicta legion across Europe to Britain, where the story of Romulus segues cleverly into that of King Arthur at the battle of Mount Badon.

What lifts this international bestseller about Romulus Augustulus above the conventional – if one can speak of such with regard to the later Roman Empire – is that Manfredi is a professor of classical archaeology. As a result, this most entertaining romp has an authenticity in background detail and colour that comes from an absolute understanding of late antiquity – as well as numerous in-jokes. The heroes encounter numerous authentic historical characters; and action takes place in recognisable archaeological sites, such as the water cistern at Misenum mentioned in Chapter 3 or the impressive Roman amphitheatre to be seen today at Caerleon in Wales.

Since the worldwide success of *Gladiator* in 2000 there have been several attempts to bring the ancient world to the big screen. Most recent is Doug Leffler's big budget film of the book *The Last Legion* with Thomas Sangster as Romulus Augustulus, which was filmed towards the end of 2005 and is due for release in January 2007. Naturally, part of the reason is that each new cinema generation reinvents every genre for itself, but a more prosaic one is that it can be profitable. The success of Peter Jackson's *Lord of the Rings* films makes swords and sandals epics not quite the box office poison they once were.

This not to say that Hollywood's forays into the past are not anticipated with slight and justifiable nervousness. It does not have a great historical track record with the ancient world, especially with late antiquity, which seems to have been in vogue in recent years. Take *King Arthur*, for example. This 2004 film is set in Britain as Stilicho withdraws the legions and provides one interpretation for the historical background of Arthur as a Roman soldier. Director Antoine Fuqua does capture both the sense of loss for an empire and the hand-to-mouth existence of splintering communities, but the film was not a great success. It was (only slightly unfairly) described by one critic as a dreadful slice of 'would-be war porn'.[20]

Better is 2001's *Attila*, a made-for-television film starring Gerard Butler as the Hun leader. Within the form's constraints, it shows an attempt at characterisation that goes beyond the two-dimensional. It certainly passes what Cambridge professor of classics Mary Beard calls the 'dormouse test' (the length of time in a Roman film before someone lying down at a dinner table asks: 'Can I pass you a stuffed dormouse?').[21] Despite the B-movie dialogue and the historical liberties taken, it reflects the factional plotting in Rome and Constantinople rather well.

But what makes the film worthy of more than a footnote is the portrayal of Romulus Augustulus' father, played by the young British actor Andrew Pleavin. His interpretation of Attila's chief-of-staff comes close to capturing Orestes' outsider status as a Roman in the Hun's court, which is underlined by Pleavin's English rather than by the mid-western accent. Orestes comes across as much more measured than his Hun colleagues, the honest voice of reason.

*   *   *

When Europe fell silent on Armistice Day 1918, classical historians began to see a modern piquancy to the fall of the Roman Empire. As the Hapsburgs, Hohenzollerns and Romanoffs became mythologised, retired and dead, sometimes all three simultaneously, it was repeatedly asked whether any lessons might be learned from the fall of the Roman Empire.[22]

But almost ninety years have passed since then and the differences seem starker than the similarities. Romulus Augustulus was not assassinated like Tsar Nicholas II; and although the Hohenzollerns and Hapsburgs too suffered exile, one to Holland and the other to Madeira, the young emperor's regalia sits as uncomfortably on the shoulders of Kaiser Wilhelm II as it does on those of Emperor Karl I.

Events have come full circle. In recent memory, the Roman Empire has never appeared – or at least never been portrayed – as so relevant to modern society as it does today. The *Senatus Populusque Romana* have become the yardstick against which contemporary society and politics are measured. The British Member of Parliament and journalist Boris Johnson has compared the unloved European Union unfavourably with the

aspirational united Europe of *pax Romana*. On the other side
of the Atlantic, the historian Harold James has considered what
he dubs 'the Roman dilemma'. This he defines as the paradoxical
notion that while global society depends on a system of rules for
building peace and prosperity, it is a system that leads inevitably
to domestic disputes, international rivalry and even war.[23]

While a dissection of the Roman Empire's body politic is
illuminating, the fall of Rome has an especially contemporary
frisson. At a basic level, analogies can be drawn between the
anomie of the iPod listener and ascetics like Simeon Stylites up his
pillar in Syria, both removed from society in contemplation of
their own gods; or the way that the theosophic rituals of the
fourth and fifth centuries herald today's dream-catchers and
crystals.

These are not just the familiar cavils of a society in decline. As I
write, the front pages of virtually every Western newspaper are
filled with soul-searching over how secular, democratic nations
should react to militant factions within Islam. Many characterise
them as, effectively, barbarians from the East – a reaction that
would have resonated fifteen centuries ago. All too many
commentators recall Edward Gibbon's warning against the
'triumph of barbarism and superstition'. Certainly some of the
most vocal and vigorous debates in Western Europe over the past
decade have been those on immigration and integration.
Depending on the paper's political hue, the answer to the
conundrum is entrenchment or accommodation. It is an issue that
can still decide the fate of governments. We have seen our
Ricimers; we have also seen our Stilichos.

As in the Europe of the fifth and sixth centuries, the
contemporary Continent has become increasingly introspective.
Reeling from an unseen terror, governments are embracing the
parochial while paying mere lip service to the creed of
globalisation. Parallels are thrown up with the desire for self-

governance in areas of Europe such as Scotland, Wales, Flanders, Wallonia, the Basque country and Catalonia, and more broadly the growing importance of regional self-expression seen in the renaissance of fringe languages such as Gaelic, Welsh, Cornish, Breton and Basque.

This brings us naturally to the much-discussed theme of the United States as the Roman Empire. Analogising the contemporary United States to the late Roman Empire has become a commonplace. The cultural historian Morris Berman is one of the most vocal. He sees a nation fat on useless consumption, saturated with corporate ideology; a culturally dulled empire, saddled with huge deficits and a hollowed-out economy. Berman himself compared the shock of the bombing of the World Trade Center in New York on 11 September 2001 to the Roman defeat at the battle of Adrianople. In much the same way as the Roman Empire's response to incomers was one of blank incomprehension and barely veiled racism, so too 'America views Islamic terrorism as completely irrational; there is no understanding of the political context of this activity'.[24]

This is going too far. It is in the entropic nature of empires, whether Egyptian, Greek, Roman, Frankish, Portuguese or British, to collapse. The very fact of the debate about Romulus Augustulus' significance and the date of the fall of the empire is significant in itself, and of course it is hysterical to suggest that the friction with Islam, confusion over globalisation or any other single reason will cause the collapse of Western society.

Romulus Augustulus shows us that it is rarely a single cataclysm that causes an implosion; instead, it is always a slow process of decline over time. Romulus remains a symbol of a world that has been lost. He is the point, the signifier from which it is possible to look back and recognise that the empire was over. The East did a much better job at realising the significance of the young emperor the first time round. The question that the West must ask itself is whether it would recognise Romulus this time if he were to come again.

When reading the apocalyptic poetic masterpiece 'Second Coming', few spare a thought for W.B. Yeats's falconer as anarchy is loosed upon the world. Romulus Augustulus is important, precisely because he was the last to see the falcon fly off the glove, to hear the tinkle of its bells grow fainter and fainter. What had been the empire founded by Romulus and built by Augustus was now something else. 'And with that', to quote the valedictory line from Dürrenmatt's play, 'the Roman Empire has ceased to exist.'

Notes

Introduction

1. For the embassy, see Malchus, fr. 14 in R.C. Blockley, *Fragmentary Classicizing Historians of the Later Roman Empire* (Liverpool: Francis Cairns, 1981–3), pp. 419–20; Zosimus, *New History*, 2.35 (there remains no satisfactory English translation of Zosimus' work, the best available is the French edition, *Zosime: Histoire Nouvelle*, trans. F. Paschoud (Paris: Budé, 1971)); Jordanes, *The Gothic History of Jordanes*, trans. Charles Mierow (Oxford: Oxford University Press, 1915), p. 143; for description of Odovacer, Eugippius, *The Life of St Severinus*, trans. Ludwig Bieler (Washington, DC: Catholic University of America Press, 1965), 7; the comment on Zeno from W.D. Burgess, 'Isaurian Factions in the Reign of Zeno the Isaurian', *Latomus* 51 (1992), 875; for a description of Byzantium, see the papers on the archaeology of Byzantium collected from the Fabric in the City Symposium and gathered in *Dumbarton Oaks Papers* 54 (2000); for the description of the imperial insignia, see Flavius Cresconius Corippus, *In laudem Iustini Augusti minoris*, trans. Averil Cameron (London: Athalone Press, 1976), p. 96.
2. Cited by John Julius Norwich in *Byzantium: The Early Centuries* (London: Penguin, 1990), p. 25.
3. 'Et quia pulcher erat', *Anonymous Valesianus*, in Ammianus Marcellinus, *Rerum gestarum libri*, vol. 3, 38.
4. Count Marcellinus, *The Chronicle of Marcellinus: A Translation and Commentary*, ed. and trans. Brian Croke (Sydney: Australian Association for Byzantine Studies, 1995), 476.
5. J.B. Bury, *History of the Later Roman Empire: From the Death of Theodosius I to the Death of Justinian*, vol. 1 (New York: Dover, 1958), p. 408; Averil Cameron, *The Mediterranean World in Late Antiquity: AD 395–600* (London: Routledge, 1993), p. 33; Brian Croke, 'AD 476: The Manufacture of a Turning Point', *Chiron* 13 (1983), 81–119.
6. Thomas Hodgkin, *Theodoric the Goth* (London: G.P. Putnam, 1891), p. 103.

7. G.W. Bowersock, Peter Brown and Oleg Grabar, *Late Antiquity. A Guide to the Postclassical World* (Cambridge, MA: Harvard University Press, 1999), p. ix.
8. Bryan Ward-Perkins, *The Fall of Rome and the End of Civilization* (Oxford: Oxford University Press, 2005), p. 82.
9. Eugippius, *Life of St Severinus*, 25.10. The statement that the West was collapsing, 'So long as the Roman dominion lasted', 20.1.
10. Sidonius Apollinaris, *Poems and Letters*, trans. W.B. Anderson, vols 1–2 (London: Loeb, 1963–5), 7.7.
11. R.W. Burgess (ed. and trans.), *The Chronicle of Hydatius and the Consularia Constantinopolitana: Two Contemporary Accounts of the Final Years of the Roman Empire* (Oxford: Clarendon Press, 1993), pp. 75, 83.
12. E.A. Thompson, 'Gildas and the History of Britain', *Britannia* 10 (1979), 208.
13. Gildas, *The Ruin of Britain and Other Works*, trans. Michael Winterbottom (London: Phillimore, 1978), 24–5. The Psalm is 44:11.
14. Bryan Ward-Perkins, *From Classical Antiquity to the Middle Ages: Urban Public Building in Northern and Central Italy AD 300–850* (Oxford: Oxford University Press, 1984), pp. 44–6; Kevin Greene, *The Archaeology of the Roman Economy* (Berkeley: University of California Press, 1986), pp. 105–8.
15. Ward-Perkins, *The Fall of Rome*, p. 106.
16. Salvian, *On the Government of God*, trans. Eva Sandford (New York: Columbia University Press, 1930), 6.18.
17. Sidonius Apollinaris, *Poems and Letters*, 8.2.
18. James O'Donnell, review of Cassiodorus, *Variae*, ed. and trans. S.J.B. Barnish (Liverpool: Liverpool University Press, 1992), in *Bryn Mawr Classical Review*, 18 April 2003.
19. Jordanes, *Romana*, 388, in Jordanes, *Romana et Getica*, ed. Theodor Mommsen, in *Monumenta Germaniae Historica, Anctorum Antiquissimorum* (Berlin: Weidmann, 1882), vol. 5.1, p. 52.

Chapter One

1. Jerome, *The Principal Works of St Jerome*, ed. Philip Schaff (New York: Christian Literature Publishing, 1892), Letters 127.12.

2. Olympiodorus, fr.11.3, in Blockley, *Fragmentary Classicizing Historians*, p. 169; Procopius, *History of the Wars*, trans. H.B. Dewing (Cambridge: Loeb, 1914), 3.2.

3. Malcolm Bull, *The Mirror of the Gods: Classical Mythology in Renaissance Art* (London: Penguin, 2005), p. 51. Paulus Orosius, *History against the Pagans*, 7.39, in *The Seven Books of History against the Pagans*, trans. Roy Deferrari (Washington, DC: Catholic University of America Press, 1964).

4. Sozomen, *Ecclesiastical History*, ed. Philip Schaff (New York: Christian Literature Publishing, 1886), 9.9; Jerome, *Letters*, 127.13.

5. Jerome, *Letters*, 128.4; *Preface to Ezekiel*, 3.

6. M. Bang, 'Expansion of the Teutons', in *The Cambridge Medieval History*, ed. H.M. Gwatkin and J.P. Whitney (Cambridge: Cambridge University Press, 1924), pp. 183–217.

7. Ammianus Marcellinus, *Rerum gestarum libri*, 3 vols, trans. J.C. Rolfe (London: Loeb, 1935–40), 31.13.2.

8. *Ibid.*, 31.13.1.

9. *Ibid.*, 31.16.7.

10. St Ambrose, *On the decease of his brother Satyrus*, 1.30, in *Some of the Principal Works of St Ambrose*, ed. Phillip Schaff (New York: Christian Literature Publishing, 1890); Libanius, *Selected Orations*, vol. 1, trans. A.F. Norman (Cambridge: Loeb, 1969), Oration 24.16. Both are examined, along with other examples, in Noel Lenski, 'Initium mali Romano imperio: Contemporary reactions to the Battle of Adrianople', *Transactions of the American Philological Association* 127 (1974), 129–69.

11. Eunapius, fr.42, in Blockley, *Fragmentary Classicizing Historians*, p. 61; Ammianus Marcellinus, *Rerum gestarum libri*, 31.4.6. He is quoting Virgil.

12. Ammianus Marcellinus, *Rerum gestarum libri*, 31.2.2; Jerome, *Letters*, 60.16.

13. Peter Brown, *The World of Late Antiquity* (London: Thames & Hudson, 1971), p. 122; Theodosian Code, 7.13.10, *The Theodosian Code and Novels and the Sirmondian Constitutions*, trans. Clyde Pharr (Princeton: Princeton University Press, 1952).

14. Ammianus Marcellinus, *Rerum gestarum libri*, 31.4.11.

15. Peter Heather, *Fall of the Roman Empire* (London: Macmillan, 2005), p. 185.

16. Themistius, Oration 16.211a–b, translated in David Potter, *The Roman Empire at Bay, AD 180–395* (London: Routledge, 2004), p. 549; Pacatus, *Panegyric to the Emperor Theodosius*, trans. C.E.V. Nixon (Liverpool: Liverpool University Press, 1987), 22.3–4.

17. Orosius, *Against the Pagans*, trans. Deferrari, 7.37.

18. Sidonius Apollinaris, *Poems and Letters*, 5.5; Gregory the Great, Selected Epistles of Gregory the Great (Books IX–XIV), ed. Philip Schaff (New York: Christian Literature Publishing, 1898), Letters 13.31.

19. Thomas Burns, *Barbarians within the Gates of Rome: A Study of Roman Military Policy and the Barbarians, ca 375–425 AD* (Bloomington: Indiana University Press, 1994), p. 20.

20. Olympiodorus, fr.38, in Blockley, *Fragmentary Classicizing Historians*, p. 201.

21. Jerome, *Letters*, 123.17.

22. John O'Flynn, *Generalissimos of the Western Roman Empire* (Edmonton: University of Alberta Press, 1983), p. xi.

23. Augustine, *Concerning the City of God against the Pagans*, trans. Henry Bettenson (London: Penguin, 1984), 5.23; Orientius, *Commonitorium*, 2.182–4 in J.N. Hillgarth (ed.), *Christianity and Paganism, 350–750* (Philadelphia, PA: University of Pennsylvania Press, 1986), p. 71.

24. Heather, *Fall of the Roman Empire*, p. 219.

25. Jerome, *Letters*, 133.9. For more on Constantine III see J.F. Drinkwater, 'The Usurpers Constantine III (407–411) and Jovinus (411–413)', *Britannia* 29 (1998), 269–98.

26. Zosimus, *New History*, 5.29.9; John Matthews, *Western Aristocracies and Imperial Court, AD 364–425* (Oxford: Clarendon Press, 1990), p. 282.

27. Gregory of Tours, *The History of the Franks*, trans. Lewis Thorpe (London: Penguin, 1974), 2.8.

28. O'Flynn, *Generalissimos of the Western Roman Empire*, p. 81; Flavius Merobaudes, *Panegyric I*, in Frank Clover, 'Flavius Merobaudes: Translation and a Historical Commentary', *Transactions of the American Philosophical Society* 61 (1971), 12–13; and for a discussion see p. 38.

29. Peter Heather, 'The Huns and the End of the Roman Empire', *English Historical Review* 110 (1995), 25; Procopius, *History of the Wars*, 3.3.15.

30. Claudian, *The Gothic Wars,* trans. Maurice Platnauer (London: Loeb, 1922), 416–18. For continuation on Hadrian's Wall see K.R. Dark, 'A Sub-Roman Re-defence of Hadrian's Wall?', *Britannia* 23 (1992), 111–20.
31. Gildas, *The Ruin of Britain,* 16; Sidonius Apollinaris, *Poems and Letters,* 8.9, 8.6; Zosimus, *New History,* 6.10.2; Honorius 16, *Chronicle of 452,* in Steven Muhlberger, 'The Gallic Chronicle of 452 and its Authority for British Events', *Britannia* 14 (1983), 31.
32. Gildas, *The Ruin of Britain,* 19; A.S. Esmonde Cleary, *The Ending of Roman Britain* (London: Batsford, 1989), p. 139; Christopher Snyder, *An Age of Tyrants: Britain and the Britons* AD *400–600* (Stroud: Sutton, 1998), p. 70.
33. William Hornsby and R. Stanton, 'The Roman Fort at Huntcliffe, near Saltburn', *Journal of Roman Studies* 2 (1912), 215–32; William Hornsby and John Laverick, 'The Roman Signal Station at Goldsborough, near Whitby, York', *Archaeological Journal* 89 (1932), 203–19.
34. Gildas, *The Ruin of Britain,* 23; Sally White *et al.,* 'A Mid-fifth-century Hoard of Roman and Pseudo-Roman Material for Patching, West Sussex', *Britannia* 30 (1999), 301–15.
35. Gildas, *The Ruin of Britain,* 25.
36. Kurt Hunter-Mann, 'The Last of the Romans: The Life and Times of Ambrosius Aurelianus', *The Heroic Age* 4 (2001), e-journal http://www.mun.ca/mst/heroicage/issues/4/Hunter-Mann.html; Geoffrey of Monmouth, *History of the Kings of Britain,* trans. Lewis Thorpe (London: Penguin, 1966), 6.5, 6.19.
37. Novels of Valentinian, 34.4, *The Theodosian Code and Novels and the Sirmondian Constitutions.*
38. *Theodosian Code,* 11.28.2–14.
39. Salvian, *On the Government of God,* 4.6; Paulus Orosius, *The Seven Books of History against the Pagans,* trans. Roy Deferrari (Washington, DC: Catholic University of America Press, 1964), 7.41.7.
40. Count Marcellinus, *The Chronicle of Marcellinus,* 447.
41. John Man, *Attila: The Barbarian King who Challenged Rome* (London: Bantam, 2005), p. 102.
42. Priscus, fr.22.3, in Blockley, *Fragmentary Classicizing Historians,* p. 315.
43. Priscus, fr.3, in *ibid.,* p. 237.

Chapter Two

1. Procopius, *History of the Wars*, 5.1.2.
2. Barry Baldwin, 'Priscus of Panium', *Byzantion* 50 (1980), 24.
3. Jordanes, *Getica*, 182.
4. Priscus, fr.11.2, in Blockley, *Fragmentary Classicizing Historians*, p. 277.
5. Heather, *Fall of the Roman Empire*, p. 323.
6. Jordanes, *Getica*, 182; Sidonius Apollinaris, *Poems and Letters*, 7.320.
7. Sidonius Apollinaris, *Poems and Letters*, 7.329–30; Jordanes, *Getica*, 191.
8. Sidonius Apollinaris, *Poems and Letters*, 8.15.
9. Jordanes, *Getica*, 207
10. Procopius, *History of the Wars*, 3.4.30–5; Jordanes, *Getica*, 221.
11. Jordanes, *Getica*, 222; R.W. Burgess (ed. and trans.), *The Chronicle of Hydatius and the Consularia Constantinopolitana: Two Contemporary Accounts of the Final Years of the Roman Empire* (Oxford: Clarendon Press, 1993), p. 103.
12. Jordanes, *Getica*, 254–5. Traditions that he was murdered by a knife-wielding Ildico come later. Count Marcellinus, *The Chronicle of Marcellinus*, 454.
13. *Anonymous Valesianus*, in Ammianus Marcellinus, *Rerum gestarum libri*, vol. 3, 38.
14. Sidonius Apollinaris, *Poems and Letters*, 7.359; Hodgkin, *Theodoric the Goth*, p. 94.
15. Procopius, *History of the Wars*, 3.4.28.
16. Count Marcellinus, *The Chronicle of Marcellinus*, 454.
17. Procopius, *History of the Wars*, 3.7.16–17.
18. Count Marcellinus, *The Chronicle of Marcellinus*, 464.
19. Novels of Majorian, 1, in *The Theodosian Code*, p. 551.
20. This is confirmed by Procopius, *History of the Wars*, 5.1.2. The word he uses to describe Romulus (μειρακιον) is generally taken to be a boy under the age of 14.
21. Leo the Great, *Letters*, trans. Edmund Hunt (New York: Fathers of the Church, 1957), Letter 159.
22. 'They were making this embassy from Patavio, a city in Noricum', Priscus, fr.11.3, line 326, in Blockley, *Fragmentary Classicizing Historians*, p. 263.

23. This passage in Victor Tonnennensis' chronicle s.a. 473 is discussed in Geoffrey Nathan, 'The Last Emperor: The Fate of Romulus Augustulus' *Classica et Mediaevalia* 43 (1992), 270, n. 28, though I come to a different conclusion.

24. Ennodius, *Life of Epiphanius*, 54; for Anthemius, see Ammianus Marcellinus *Rerum gestarum libri*, 17.9.3; for Julian, see John O'Flynn, 'A Greek on the Roman Throne: The Fate of Anthemius', *Historia* 40 (1991), 123.

25. Sidonius Apollinaris, *Poems and Letters*, 1.9.

26. Priscus, fr.65, in Blockley, *Fragmentary Classicizing Historians*, pp. 373–5.

27. Count Marcellinus, *Chronicle of Marcellinus*, 473; Ennodius, *Life of Epiphanius*, 79.

28. Sidonius Apollinaris, *Poems and Letters*, 2.1.

29. *Ibid.*, 6.12.

30. *Ibid.*, 3.3.

31. Ausonius, *The Order of Famous Cities*, in *Ausonius*, vol. 1, trans. Evelyn White (London: Loeb, 1919), 20.39–40.

32. Jill Harries, *Sidonius Apollinaris and the Fall of Rome*, AD 407–485 (Oxford: Oxford University Press, 1994), p. 231. Sidonius Apollinaris, *Poems and Letters*, 5.16, 5.6.

33. Sidonius Apollinaris, *Poems and Letters*, 7.7.

34. Ennodius, *Life of Epiphanius*, 95.

35. *Auct. Haun. ordinis post. margo*, 475, in Mommsen (ed.), *Chronica Minora*, vol. 1, in *Monumenta Germaniae Historica, Auctores Antiquissimi*, vol. 9, p. 307; O'Flynn, *Generalissimos of the Western Roman Empire*, p. 134.

36. *Auct. Haun. ordinis post. margo*, 475, in Mommsen, *Chronica Minora*, p. 309; *Anonymous Valesianus*, 36.

37. Robert Adam, *Ruins of the Palace of the Emperor Diocletian at Spalatro in Dalmatia* (London: printed for the author, 1764).

38. Strabo, *Geography*, 5.1.7; Jordanes, *Getica*, 29; Pliny, *Natural History*, 9.79.

39. Sidonius Apollinaris, *Poems and Letters*, 1.5; Martial, *Epigrams*, 3.56.

40. Pliny, *Natural History*, 30.6.18.

41. Sidonius Apollinaris, *Poems and Letters*, 1.8.

42. *Auctarii Haun. ordo prior*, 476, in Theodor Mommsen (ed.),

Chronica Minora Saec. iv, v, vi, vii, vols 1 and 2, in *Monumenta Germaniae Historica, Auctores Antiquissimi*, vol. 9 (Berlin: Weidmann, 1892–4), p. 309. I have translated the phrase loosely. The literal Latin translation is 'external defences', but this seems too narrow a sense for the power Orestes actually wielded. Penny MacGeorge, *Late Roman Warlords* (Oxford: Oxford University Press, 2002), p. 280, n. 45, ingeniously proposes that 'external' refers to anything outside the imperial palace.

43. Procopius, *History of the Wars*, 5.1.4.

44. For land grants throughout the empire see G.E.M. de Ste Croix, *The Class Struggle in the Ancient Greek World* (London: Duckworth, 1983), appendix 3; S.J.B. Barnish, 'Taxation, Land and Barbarian Settlement in the Western Empire', *Papers of the British School at Rome* 54 (1986), 170–95; Herwig Wolfram, *History of the Goths* (London: University of California Press, 1988), pp. 296–7.

45. Contrast J. O'Flynn, *Generalissimos of the Western Roman Empire* (Edmonton: University of Alberta Press, 1983*)*, p. 135, with MacGeorge, *Late Roman Warlords*, p. 282.

46. Eugippius, *Life of St Severinus*, 7: I am not convinced that the Odovacar [*sic*] referred to by Gregory of Tours (2.18) is the same man.

47. Procopius, *History of the Wars*, 6.12.32.

48. Dirk Henning, *Periclitans res public: Kaisertum und Eliten in der Krise des Weströmischen Reiches 454/5–493 n. Chr.* (Stuttgart: Franz Steiner, 1999), p. 60.

49. Ennodius, *Life of Epiphanius*, 12–13.

50. Cassiodorus, *Chronica*, 476, in Mommsen, *Chronica Minora*, pp. 158–9.

51. *Anonymous Valesianus*, 38.

Chapter Three

1. Cicero, *Letters to Atticus*, 2.8.2; Propertius refers to little dinghies powered by paddles, in *Elegies*, 1.11; Horace, *Satires*, 2.4.33.

2. Martial, *Epigrams*, 1.62; Seneca, *Ad Lucilium Epistulae Morales*, 51; Augustine, *Contra Academicos*, 2.2.6.

3. Chester Starr, *The Roman Imperial Navy; 31 BC to AD 324* (New York: Cornell University Press, 1941), pp. 13–21.

4. Pliny the Younger, *Letters*, 6.16, 20.

5. Jordanes, *Getica*, 242.
6. Although the identification between Romulus' place of exile and a villa of Lucullus is certain, there remains considerable disagreement over whether Marius' estate and this estate of Lucullus are one and the same. For a summary of the argument see Arthur Keaveney, *Lucullus: A Life* (London York: Routledge, 1992), pp. 148–9. Plutarch, *Marius*, 34; Pliny, *Natural History*, 18.32.
7. Garrett Fagan, 'Sergius Orata: Inventor of the Hypocaust?', *Phoenix* 50 (1996), 56–66.
8. Plutarch, *Lucullus*, 39; Pliny, *Natural History*, 9.170.
9. Pope Silvester, *The Book of the Pontiffs*, trans. Raymond Davis (Liverpool: Liverpool University Press, 1989), p. 26.
10. Domenico Comparetti, *Virgil in the Middle Ages*, trans. E.F.M. Benecke (Princeton: Princeton University Press, 1996), p. 269.
11. Bury, *History of the Later Roman Empire*, p. 405.
12. John Kent, 'Julius Nepos and the Fall of the Western Empire', in *Corolla Numismatica Memoriae Erich Swoboda Dedicata* (Cologne: Hermann Böhlaus, 1966), p. 146.
13. Nathan, 'The Last Emperor: The Fate of Romulus Augustulus', 261–71.
14. See Cassiodorus, *Variae*, 8.25 and notes in *The Letters of Cassiodorus*, trans. Thomas Hodgkin (London: Henry Frowde, 1886), p. 374.
15. Nathan, 'The Last Emperor: The Fate of Romulus Augustulus', 264.
16. Eugippius, *Life of St Severinus*, 40.
17. The analogy of Severinus as a cowboy is too good not to use and is shamelessly stolen from the residential address delivered by James O'Donnell, at the 135th meeting of the American Philological Association in San Francisco, 4 January 2004.
18. Eugippius, *Life of St Severinus*, 28.
19. *Ibid.*, 30.
20. *Ibid.*, 20.
21. *Ibid.*, 24.
22. *Ibid.*, 44.
23. *Ibid.*, 46.
24. Eugippius, *Epistula ad Paschasium*, 8.
25. Adrian Murdoch, *The Last Pagan* (Stroud: Sutton, 2005), pp. 19–20.

26. MacGeorge, *Late Roman Warlords*, pp. 195–6.
27. Eugippius, *Life of St Severinus*, 46.
28. Gregory the Great, *Letters*, 3.1, cf. 9.181 and 11.19. For Willibald, Huneberc (properly Hygeburg) of Heidenheim, see *The Hodoeporican of St Willibald*, 172, in C.H. Talbot, *The Anglo-Saxon Missionaries in Germany* (London: Sheed and Ward, 1954), p. 172.
29. Jordanes, *Getica*, 234; Count Marcellinus, *Chronicle of Marcellinus*, 477; *Auctarii Haun. ordo prior*, 477, in *Chronica Minora*, p. 311. For the hoard see Barbara Deppert-Lippitz, 'A Late Antique Crossbow Fibula in the Metropolitan Museum of Art', *Metropolitan Museum Journal* 35 (2000), 58–9.
30. Cassiodorus, *Variae*, 5.41.
31. Alastair Small and Robert Buck, *The Excavations of San Giovanni di Ruoti* (Cheektowaga: University of Toronto Press, 1994).
32. Procopius, *History of the Wars*, 6.6.17.
33. For details see 'Odovacer', in A.H.M. Martin, *Prosopography of the Later Roman Empire* (Cambridge: Cambridge University Press, 1971), vol. 2, p. 793.
34. *Auctarii Haun. ordo prior*, 480, in Mommsen, *Chronica Minora*, p. 311; for the rumour that Glycerius was involved in the murder of Julius Nepos, see Malchus, fr.1, in Blockley, *Fragmentary Classicizing Historians*, p. 403. '[Nepos] was killed as the result of a plot by Glycerius.'
35. John Moorhead, *Theoderic in Italy* (Oxford: Clarendon Press, 1992), p. 10.
36. Géza Alföldy, *Noricum* (London: Routledge & Kegan Paul, 1974), p. 226.
37. Agnellus of Ravenna, *The Book of the Pontiffs of the Church of Ravenna*, trans. Deborah Maukopf Deliyannis (Washington, DC: Catholic University of America Press, 2004), Peter the Elder, 94. With the victory I have followed the account of Michael McCormick, 'Odovacer, Emperor Zeno and the Rugian Victory Legation', *Byzantion* 47 (1977), 212–22.
38. Procopius, *History of the Wars*, 6.6.16.
39. Malchus, fr.18, in Blockley, *Fragmentary Classicizing Historians*, p. 429.
40. Ennodius, *Der Theoderich-Pannegyricus des Ennodius*, trans. Christian Rohr (Hannover: Hahnsche Buchhandlung, 1995), p. 26. See also Procopius, *History of the Wars*, 5.1.12.

41. Ennodius, *Der Theoderich-Pannegyricus des Ennodius*, 33; James O'Donnell, 'Liberius the Patrician', *Traditio* 37 (1981), 36.
42. Ennodius, *Der Theoderich-Pannegyricus des Ennodius*, 39–47.
43. Ennodius, *Life of Epiphanius*, 112–13.
44. Mark Johnson, 'Towards a History of Theoderic's Building Program', *Dumbarton Oaks Papers* 42 (1988), 78, n. 63.
45. Jordanes, *Getica*, 293.
46. *Anonymous Valesianus*, 53.
47. John of Antioch, fr.214a, in C.D. Gordon, *The Age of Attila: Fifth-Century Byzantium and the Barbarians* (Ann Arbor: University of Michigan Press, 1966), pp. 182–3.

Chapter Four

1. Procopius, *History of the Wars*, 5.9.
2. Ennodius, *Der Theoderich-Pannegyricus des Ennodius*, 93.
3. *Anonymous Valesianus*, 59.
4. Moorhead, *Theoderic in Italy*, p. 252, n. 2.
5. *Anonymous Valesianus*, 79.
6. Jordanes, *Getica*, 281.
7. Moorhead, *Theoderic in Italy*, p. 28, n. 109; Cassiodorus, *Variae*, 1.3.
8. 'Foreign people', legend on the reverse of the Senigallia medal; Cassiodorus, *Variae*, 2.40.
9. For wearing Romulus Augustulus' ornaments see *Anonymous Valesianus*, 64; for the purple worn by Romulus see Pliny, *Natural History*, 9.63; for Theoderic wearing the purple see Cassiodorus, *Variae*, 1.2; Letter to Anastasius, Cassiodorus, *Variae*, 1.1.
10. Ward-Perkins, *The Fall of Rome and the End of Civilization*, p. 73.
11. I follow Moorhead's suggestion, Moorhead, *Theoderic in Italy*, though see p. 60, n. 113, for counter-arguments.
12. *Life of Fulgentius*, 9, in Fulgentius, *Selected Works*, trans. Robert Eno (Washington, DC: Catholic University of America Press, 1997).
13. Cassiodorus, *Variae*, 1.25.
14. *Ibid.*, 7.6; 3.30.
15. *Ibid.*, 3.31; 7.6; 2.35.
16. *Ibid.*, 4.51.
17. The account is taken from Johnson, 'Towards a History of Theoderic's Building Program', 73–96.

18. *Ibid.*, 76; Cassiodorus, *Variae*, 6.7.3.
19. *Anonymous Valesianus*, 70; Cassiodorus, *Variae*, 9.3, 3.25, 4.30, 2.23.
20. Cassiodorus, *Variae*, 10.27; *Anonymous Valesianus*, 73.
21. Cassiodorus, *Variae*, 3.41, 10.27.
22. For the number of Romans in government see P.S. Barnwell, *Emperor, Prefects and Kings: The Roman West, 395–565* (London: Duckworth, 1992), p. 155; Cassiodorus' father, *Variae*, 1.4; for Liberius I have broadly followed the account of O'Donnell, 'Liberius the Patrician', 31–72.
23. Cassiodorus, *Variae*, 2.16; Procopius, *History of the Wars*, 5.4.24.
24. O'Donnell, 'Liberius the Patrician', 36–7.
25. Cassiodorus, *Variae*, 2.16; Murdoch, *The Last Pagan*, pp. 68–9.
26. See 'Petrus Marcellinus Felix Liberius', PLRE 2, pp. 677–81; Cassiodorus, *Variae*, 2.16.
27. The connection with the Romulus of the letter and Romulus Augustulus is by no means absolute, but has been generally accepted as such since *The Letters of Cassiodorus* (trans. Hodgkin), pp. 215–16. Certainly it was a rare name in late antiquity. PLRE 2 mentions six, one of whom is the emperor, another his grandfather.
28. Cassiodorus, *Variae*, 3.35. The translation is based on that of Nathan, 'The Last Emperor: The Fate of Romulus Augustulus', 269, with minor changes.
29. 'Theodorus 62', PLRE 2, p. 1097; Fulgentius, *Selected Works*, Letter 6.1.
30. Cassiodorus, *Variae*, 2.27.
31. *Anonymous Valesianus*, 83.
32. Pope John, *The Book of the Pontiffs*, p. 50.
33. Moorhead, *Theodoric in Italy*, p. 68.
34. Cassiodorus, *Variae*, 2.16.5; Sidonius Apollinaris, *Poems and Letters*, 7.14; Cassiodorus, *Variae*, 10.1. For several other examples see John Moorhead, 'Italian Loyalties during Justinian's Gothic War', *Byzantion* 53 (1983), 575–96, specifically 577.
35. Cassiodorus, *Variae*, 12.5.4; see Peter Heather, 'Theoderic, King of the Goths', *Early Medieval Europe* (1995), 156, for a map of the distribution of Gothic cemeteries.
36. *Theodosian Code*, 3.14.
37. Theudis, PLRE 2, p. 1112–13; *Anonymous Valesianus*, 61.

38. Moorhead, *Theodoric in Italy*, p. 220.
39. *Anonymous Valesianus*, 85.
40. Boethius, *The Consolation of Philosophy*, trans. V.E. Watts (London: Penguin, 1969), 1.4.89–94.
41. Moorhead, *Theodoric in Italy*, pp. 220–1.
42. *Anonymous Valesianus*, 87.
43. Procopius, *History of the Wars*, 5.1.35–9.
44. Edward Hutton, *The Story of Ravenna* (London: J.M. Dent, 1926), p. 4.
45. *Ibid.*, p. 34.
46. Procopius, *History of the Wars*, 8.34.
47. Corippus, *In laudem Iustini Augusti minoris*, p. 96.
48. Patrick Leigh Fermor, *A Time of Gifts* (London: Penguin, 1979), p. 174.

Chapter Five

1. *Lay of Hildebrand*, trans. Brian Murdoch, in 'Hildebrand', *Lines Review* 109 (June 1989), 20–2.
2. Brian Murdoch, 'Heroic Verse', in Brian Murdoch (ed.), *German Literature of the Early Middle Ages* (Rochester: Camden House, 2004), p. 124.
3. John Man, *Attila: The Barbarian King who Challenged Rome* (London: Bantam, 2005), specifically Chapter 12.
4. Eugène Delacroix, *Journal of Eugène Delacroix*, trans. Lucy Norton, intro. Hubert Wellington (London: Phaidon, 1995), p. xxiv.
5. Lee Johnson, *The Paintings of Eugène Delacroix: A Critical Catalogue*, vol. 5 (Oxford: Clarendon Press, 1989), p. 33.
6. Eugène Delacroix, *Selected Letters, 1813–1863*, ed. John Russell, trans. Jean Stewart (London: Eyre & Spottiswoode, 1971), p. 18.
7. Johnson, *The Paintings of Eugène Delacroix*, p. 34.
8. Norman Bryson, *Tradition and Desire* (Cambridge: Cambridge University Press, 1984), p. 177.
9. Anita Hopmans, 'Delacroix's Decorations in the Palais Bourbon Library: A Classic Example of an Unacademic Approach', *Simiolus* 17 (1987), 245.
10. Hopmans, 'Delacroix's Decorations in the Palais Bourbon Library', 248.

11. Antonio Gramsci, *Selections from Political Writings (1921–1926)*, ed. and trans. Quintin Hoare (London: Lawrence and Wishart, 1978), p. 212.
12. Not published until the 1990s in Katherine Bucknell, *In Solitude, for Company: W.H. Auden after 1940. Unpublished Prose and Recent Criticism* (Oxford: Clarendon Press, 1995), p. 120.
13. Cited in Richard Jenkyns, *The Legacy of Rome: A New Appraisal* (Oxford: Oxford University Press, 1992), p. 142.
14. Trans. Mónica de la Torre, *Boston Review* 24/6, December 1999/January 2000, p. 25.
15. Friedrich Dürrenmatt, 'Anmerkung II zu Romulus', *Theater-Schriften und Reden* (Zurich: Arche, 1966), p. 177.
16. Procopius, *History of the Wars*, 3.2.25–6.
17. Dürrenmatt, 'Anmerkung II zu Romulus', pp. 177–8.
18. Plutarch, *Lives*, trans. Bernadotte Perrin (London: Loeb, 1967), *Romulus*, 9.4–5; Livy, *Ab urbe condita*, trans. B.O. Foster (London: Loeb, 1919), 1.6–7.
19. Friedrich Lotter, *Severinus von Noricum: Legende und historische Wirklichkeit* (Stuttgart: Anton Hiersemann, 1976).
20. Tim Robey, 'Prithee, Good Sirs – No More Bloody Battle Scenes', *Daily Telegraph*, 30 July 2004.
21. Mary Beard, 'Apart from vomitoriums and orgies, what did the Romans do for us?' *Guardian*, 29 October 2005.
22. Walter Goffart, *Rome's Fall and After* (London: Hambledon Press, 1989), p. 33.
23. Boris Johnson, *The Dream of Rome* (London: HarperCollins, 2006); Harold James, *The Roman Predicament: How the Rules of International Order Create the Politics of Empire* (Princeton: Princeton University Press, 2006).
24. Morris Berman, 'Waiting for the barbarians', *Guardian*, 6 October 2001.

Select Bibliography

Primary Sources

Agnellus of Ravenna, *The Book of the Pontiffs of the Church of Ravenna*, trans. Deborah Maukopf Deliyannis, Washington, DC: Catholic University of America Press, 2004

Ammianus Marcellinus, *Rerum gestarum libri*, 3 vols, trans. J.C. Rolfe, London: Loeb, 1935–40. Vol. 3 contains the text of the *Anonymous Valesianus*

Augustine, *The Confessions and Letters of St Augustin, with a Sketch of his Life and Work*, ed. Phillip Schaff, New York: Christian Literature Publishing, 1886

——, *Concerning the City of God against the Pagans*, trans. Henry Bettenson, London: Penguin, 1984

Ausonius, *Ausonius*, vol. 1, trans. Evelyn White, London: Loeb, 1919

Blockley, R.C., *Fragmentary Classicizing Historians of the Later Roman Empire*, vols 1 and 2, Liverpool: Francis Cairns, 1981–3. Contains translations of Olympiodorus, Priscus and Malchus

Boethius, *The Consolation of Philosophy*, trans. V.E. Watts, London: Penguin, 1969

The Book of the Pontiffs, trans. Raymond Davis, Liverpool: Liverpool University Press, 1989

Burgess, R.W. (ed. and trans.), *The Chronicle of Hydatius and the Consularia Constantinopolitana: Two Contemporary Accounts of the Final Years of the Roman Empire*, Oxford: Clarendon Press, 1993

Cassiodorus, *The Letters of Cassiodorus*, trans. Thomas Hodgkin, London: Henry Frowde, 1886

——, *Variae*, ed. and trans. S.J.B. Barnish, Liverpool: Liverpool University Press, 1992

Claudian, *Claudian*, trans. Maurice Platnauer, London: Loeb, 1922

Clover, Frank, 'Flavius Merobaudes: Translation and a Historical Commentary', *Transactions of the American Philosophical Society* 61 (1971), 1–78

Count Marcellinus, *The Chronicle of Marcellinus: A Translation and Commentary*, ed. and trans. Brian Croke, Sydney: Australian Association for Byzantine Studies, 1995

Cresconius Corippus, Flavius, *In laudem Iustini Augusti minoris*, trans. Averil Cameron, London: Athalone Press, 1976

Deferrari, Roy, *Early Christian Biographies*, Washington, DC: Catholic University of America Press, 1952. Contains a translation of Ennodius' *Life of St Epiphanius*

Ennodius, *Der Theoderich-Panegyricus des Ennodius*, trans. Christian Rohr, Hannover: Hahnsche Buchhandlung, 1995

Eugippius, *The Life of St Severinus*, trans. Ludwig Bieler, Washington, DC: Catholic University of America Press, 1965

Fulgentius, *Selected Works*, trans. Robert Eno, Washington, DC: Catholic University of America Press, 1997

Geoffrey of Monmouth, *History of the Kings of Britain*, trans. Lewis Thorpe, London: Penguin, 1966

Gildas, *The Ruin of Britain and Other Works*, trans. Michael Winterbottom, London: Phillimore, 1978

Gordon, C.D., *The Age of Attila: Fifth-century Byzantium and the Barbarians*, Ann Arbor: University of Michigan Press, 1966

Gregory of Tours, *The History of the Franks*, trans. Lewis Thorpe, London: Penguin, 1974

Heather, Peter, and Matthews, John, *The Goths in the Fourth Century*, Liverpool: Liverpool University Press, 1991

Hillgarth, J.N. (ed.), *Christianity and Paganism, 350–750*, Philadelphia, PA: University of Pennsylvania Press, 1986

Jerome, *The Principal Works of St Jerome*, ed. Phillip Schaff, New York: Christian Literature Publishing, 1892

Jordanes, *Romana et Getica*, ed. Theodor Mommsen, in *Monumenta Germaniae Historica, Auctorum Antiquissimorum*, vol. 5.1, Berlin: Weidmann, 1882

——, *The Gothic History of Jordanes*, trans. Charles Mierow, Oxford: Oxford University Press, 1915

Lay of Hildebrand, trans. Brian Murdoch, in 'Hildebrand', *Lines Review* 109 (June 1989), 20–2

Leo the Great, *Letters*, trans. Edmund Hunt, New York: Fathers of the Church, 1957

Mommsen, Theodor (ed.), *Chronica Minora Saec. iv, v, vi, vii*, vols 1 and

2, in *Monumenta Germaniae Historica, Auctores Antiquissimi*, vol. 9, Berlin: Weidmann, 1892–4

Orosius, Paulus, *The Seven Books of History against the Pagans*, trans. Roy Deferrari, Washington, DC: Catholic University of America Press, 1964

Pacatus, *Panegyric to the Emperor Theodosius*, trans. C.E.V. Nixon, Liverpool: Liverpool University Press, 1987

Procopius, *History of the Wars*, trans. H.B. Dewing, London: Loeb, 1914–40

Salvian, *On the Government of God*, trans. Eva Sandford, New York: Columbia University Press, 1930

——, *The Writings of Salvian the Presbyter*, trans. Jeremiah O'Sullivan, Washington, DC: Catholic University of America Press, 1947

Sidonius Apollinaris, *Poems and Letters*, trans. W.B. Anderson, vols 1 and 2, London: Loeb, 1963–5

Talbot, C.H., *The Anglo-Saxon Missionaries in Germany*, London: Sheed and Ward, 1954

The Theodosian Code and Novels and the Sirmondian Constitutions, trans. Clyde Pharr, Princeton: Princeton University Press, 1952

Zosimus, *Zosime: Histoire Nouvelle*, trans. F. Paschoud, Paris: Budé, 1971

Secondary Sources

Alföldy, Géza, *Noricum*, London: Routledge & Kegan Paul, 1974

D'Arms, John, *Romans on the Bay of Naples*, Cambridge, MA: Harvard University Press, 1970

Badian, E., 'Marius' Villas: The Testimony of the Slave and the Knave', *Journal of Roman Studies* 63 (1973), 121–32

Baldwin, Barry, 'Malchus of Philadelphia', *Dumbarton Oaks Papers* 31 (1977), 91–107

——, 'Priscus of Panium', *Byzantion* 50 (1980), 18–61

Bardill, Jonathan, 'The Great Palace of the Byzantine Emperors and the Walker Trust Excavations', *Journal of Roman Archaeology* 12 (1999), 216–30

Barnish, S.J.B., 'Taxation, Land and Barbarian Settlement in the Western Empire', *Papers of the British School at Rome* 54 (1986), 170–95

——, 'Ennodius' Lives of Epiphanius and Antony: Two Models for the Christian Gentleman', *Studia Patristica* 24 (1993), 13–19

Barnwell, P.S., *Emperor, Prefects and Kings: The Roman West, 395–565*, London: Duckworth, 1992

Brown, Peter, *The World of Late Antiquity*, London: Thames & Hudson, 1971

Browning, Robert, 'Where was Attila's camp?', *Journal of Hellenic Studies* 73 (1953), 143–5

Bryson, Norman, *Tradition and Desire*, Cambridge: Cambridge University Press, 1984

Bucknell, Katherine, *In Solitude, for Company: W.H. Auden after 1940, Unpublished Prose and Recent Criticism*, Oxford: Clarendon Press, 1995

Burgess, W.D., 'Isaurian Factions in the Reign of Zeno the Isaurian', *Latomus* 51 (1992), 874–80

Burns, Thomas, *Barbarians within the Gates of Rome: A Study of Roman Military Policy and the Barbarians, ca 375–425 AD*, Bloomington: Indiana University Press, 1994

Bury, J.B., 'A Note on the Emperor Olybrius', *English Historical Review* 1 (1886) 507–9

——, *History of the Later Roman Empire: From the Death of Theodosius I to the Death of Justinian*, vols 1 and 2, New York: Dover, 1958

Cameron, Averil, *The Later Roman Empire: AD 284–430*, London: Fontana, 1993

——, *The Mediterranean World in Late Antiquity: AD 395–600*, London: Routledge, 1993

Comparetti, Domenico, *Virgil in the Middle Ages*, trans. E.F.M. Benecke, Princeton: Princeton University Press, 1996

Croke, Brian, 'Basiliscus, the Boy Emperor', *Greek, Roman and Byzantine Studies* 24 (1983), 81–91

——, 'AD 476: The Manufacture of a Turning Point', *Chiron* 13 (1983), 81–119

Dark, K.R., 'A Sub-Roman Re-defence of Hadrian's Wall?', *Britannia* 23 (1992), 111–20

Delacroix, Eugène, *Selected Letters, 1813–1863*, ed. John Russell, trans. Jean Stewart, London: Eyre & Spottiswoode, 1971

——, *Journal of Eugène Delacroix*, trans. Lucy Norton, intro. Hubert Wellington, London: Phaidon, 1995

Demougeot, Emilienne, 'Bedeutet das Jahr 476 das Ende des romischen Reichs im Okzident?', *Klio* 60 (1978), 371–81

Deppert-Lippitz, Barbara, 'A Late Antique Crossbow Fibula in the Metropolitan Museum of Art', *Metropolitan Museum Journal* 35 (2000)

Dürrenmatt, Friedrich, *Theater-Schriften und Reden*, Zurich: Arche, 1966

——, *Romulus der Große*, ed. H.F. Garten, London: Methuen, 1968

Esmonde Cleary, A.S., *The Ending of Roman Britain*, London: Batsford, 1989

Fermor, Patrick Leigh, *A Time of Gifts*, London: Penguin, 1979

Fischer, Thomas, *Noricum*, Mainz: Philip von Zabern, 2002

Goffart, Walter, *Rome's Fall and After*, London: Hambledon Press, 1989

Gramsci, Antonio, *Selections from Political Writings (1921–1926)*, ed. and trans. Quintin Hoare, London: Lawrence and Wishart, 1978

Grant, Michael, *From Rome to Byzantium: The Fifth Century AD*, London: Routledge, 1998

Greene, Kevin, *The Archaeology of the Roman Economy*, London: University of California Press, 1986

Harries, Jill, *Sidonius Apollinaris and the Fall of Rome, AD 407–485*, Oxford: Oxford University Press, 1994

Heather, Peter, *Goths and Romans*, Oxford: Oxford University Press, 1991

——, 'Theoderic, King of the Goths', *Early Medieval Europe* (1995), 145–73

——, 'The Huns and the End of the Roman Empire', *English Historical Review* 110 (1995), 4–41

——, *Fall of the Roman Empire*, London: Macmillan, 2005

Henning, Dirk, *Periclitans res public: Kaisertum und Eliten in der Krise des Weströmischen Reiches 454/5–493 n. Chr.*, Stuttgart: Franz Steiner, 1999

Hodgkin, Thomas, *Italy and her Invaders: 376–476*, vol. 2, Oxford: Clarendon, 1880

——, *Theodoric the Goth*, London: G.P. Putnam, 1891

Hopmans, Anita, 'Delacroix's Decorations in the Palais Bourbon Library: A Classic Example of an Unacademic Approach', *Simiolus* 17 (1987), 240–69

Hornsby, William and Stanton, R., 'The Roman fort at Huntcliff, near Saltburn', *Journal of Roman Studies* 2 (1912), 215–32

——, and Laverick, John, 'The Roman Signal Station at Goldsborough, near Whitby, York', *Archaeological Journal* 89 (1932), 203–19

Hunter-Mann, Kurt, 'The Last of the Romans: The Life and Times of Ambrosius Aurelianus', *The Heroic Age* 4 (2001), e-journal: http://www.mun.ca/mst/heroicage/issues/4/Hunter-Mann.html

Hutton, Edward, *The Story of Ravenna*, London: J.M. Dent, 1926

James, Dominic, 'The Golden Clasp of the Late Roman State', *Early Medieval Europe* 5 (1996), 127–53

Jenny, Urs, *Dürrenmatt: A Study of his Plays*, London: Eyre Methuen, 1978

Johnson, Lee, *The Paintings of Eugène Delacroix: A Critical Catalogue*, vol. 5, Oxford: Clarendon Press, 1989

Johnson, Mark, 'Towards a History of Theoderic's Building Program', *Dumbarton Oaks Papers* 42 (1988), 73–96

Jones, A.H.M., 'The Constitutional Position of Odovacer and Theoderic', *Journal of Roman Studies* 52 (1962), 126–30

——, *The Later Roman Empire, 284–602: A Social, Economic and Administrative Survey*, Oxford: Blackwell, 1964

Keaveney, Arthur, *Lucullus: A Life*, London and New York: Routledge, 1992

Keeley, Edmund, *Cavafy's Alexandria*, Princeton: Princeton University Press, 1976

Kelly, J.N.D., *Jerome: His Life, Writings and Controversies*, London: Duckworth, 1975

Kennell, S.A.H., *Magnus Felix Ennodius: A Gentleman of the Church*, Ann Arbor: University of Michigan Press, 2000

Kent, John, 'Julius Nepos and the Fall of the Western Empire', in *Corolla Numismatica Memoriae Erich Swoboda Dedicata*, Cologne: Hermann Böhlaus, 1966, 146–50

——, *The Roman Imperial Coinage*, vol. 10, London: Spink & Son, 1994

Krautschick, Stefan, 'Zwei Aspekte des Jahres 476', *Historia* 35 (1986), 344–71

Lenski, Noel, 'Initium mali Romano imperio: Contemporary Reactions to the Battle of Adrianople', *Transactions of the American Philological Association* 127 (1974), 129–69

Lotter, Friedrich, *Severinus von Noricum: Legende und historische Wirklichkeit*, Stuttgart: Anton Hiersemann, 1976

Macbain, Bruce, 'Odovacer the Hun?', *Classical Philology* 78 (1983), 323–7

McCormick, Michael, 'Odovacer, Emperor Zeno and the Rugian Victory Legation', *Byzantion* 47 (1977), 212–22

Select Bibliography

MacGeorge, Penny, *Late Roman Warlords*, Oxford: Oxford University Press, 2002

Man, John, *Attila: The Barbarian King who Challenged Rome*, London: Bantam, 2005

Manfredi, Valerio Massimo, *The Last Legion: A Novel*, London: Macmillan, 2003

Martin, A.H.M., *The Prosopography of the Later Roman Empire*, Cambridge: Cambridge University Press, 1971, vol. 1

Martindale, J.R., *The Prosopography of the Later Roman Empire*, vol. 2, Cambridge: Cambridge University Press, 1980

Matthews, John, 'Olympiodorus of Thebes and the History of the West (AD 407–425)', *Journal of Roman Studies* 60 (1970), 79–95

——, *Western Aristocracies and Imperial Court, AD 364–425*, Oxford: Clarendon Press, 1990

Moorhead, John, 'Italian Loyalties during Justinian's Gothic War', *Byzantion* 53 (1983), 575–96

——, *Theoderic in Italy*, Oxford: Clarendon Press, 1992

Muhlberger, Steven, 'The Gallic Chronicle of 452 and its Authority for British Events', *Britannia* 14 (1983), 23–33

——, *The Fifth-Century Chronicles: Prosper, Hydatius and the Gallic Chronicler of 452*, Leeds: Francis Cairns, 1990

Murdoch, Adrian, *The Last Pagan: Julian the Apostate and the Death of the Ancient World*, Stroud: Sutton, 2005

Murdoch, Brian, 'Heroic Verse', in *idem* (ed.), *German Literature of the Early Middle Ages*, Rochester: Camden House, 2004, 121–38

Murphy, Cullen, 'The Road from Ravenna', *Atlantic Monthly*, September 2006, 127–32

Nathan, Geoffrey, 'The Last Emperor: The Fate of Romulus Augustulus', *Classica et Mediaevalia* 43 (1992), 261–71

Norman, Frederick, *Three Essays on the Hildebrandslied*, London: University of London, 1973

Norwich, John Julius, *Byzantium: The Early Centuries*, London: Penguin, 1990

O'Donnell, James, *Cassiodorus*, London: University of California Press, 1979

——, 'Liberius the Patrician', *Traditio* 37 (1981), 31–72

——, 'The aims of Jordanes', *Historia* 31 (1982), 223–40

O'Flynn, John, *Generalissimos of the Western Roman Empire*, Edmonton: University of Alberta Press, 1983

——, 'A Greek on the Roman Throne: The Fate of Anthemius', *Historia* 40 (1991), 122–8

Popa, Opritsa, *Bibliophiles and Bibliothieves: The Search for the Hildebrandslied and the Willehalm Codex*, New York: De Gruyter, 2003

Potter, David, *The Roman Empire at Bay, AD 180–395*, London: Routledge, 2004

Raymond, Boris, *The Twelfth Vulture of Romulus*, San Jose: KLYO Press, 2003

Reece, Richard, *The Later Roman Empire: An Archaeology AD 150–600*, Stroud: Tempus, 1999

Small, Alastair, and Buck, Robert, *The Excavations of San Giovanni di Ruoti*, Cheektowaga: University of Toronto Press, 1994

Snyder, Christopher, *An Age of Tyrants: Britain and the Britons AD 400–600*, Stroud: Sutton, 1998

Spears, Monroe, *The Poetry of W.H. Auden: The Disenchanted Island*, Oxford: Oxford University Press, 1963

Starr, Chester, *The Roman Imperial Navy; 31 BC to AD 324*, New York: Cornell University Press, 1941

Thompson, E.A., 'The Camp of Attila', *Journal of Hellenic Studies* 65 (1946), 112–15

——, 'Gildas and the History of Britain', *Britannia* 10 (1979), 203–26

——, *Romans and Barbarians*, Madison: University of Wisconsin Press, 1982

——, *The Huns*, Oxford: Blackwell, 1996

Tiusanen, Timo, *Dürrenmatt: A Study in Plays, Prose, Theory*, Princeton: Princeton University Press, 1977

Trilling, James, 'The Soul of the Empire: Style and Meaning in the Mosaic Pavement of the Byzantine Imperial Palace in Constantinople', *Dumbarton Oaks Papers* 43 (1989), 27–72

Varady, Laszlo, *Epochenwechsel um 476: Odoaker, Theoderich d. Gr. und die Umwandlungen*, Bonn: Rudolf Habelt, 1984

Ward-Perkins, Bryan, *From Classical Antiquity to the Middle Ages: Urban Public Building in Northern and Central Italy AD 300–850*, Oxford: Oxford University Press, 1984

——, *The Fall of Rome and the End of Civilization*, Oxford: Oxford University Press, 2005

White, Sally, *et al.*, 'A Mid-fifth-century Hoard of Roman and Pseudo-Roman Material for Patching, West Sussex', *Britannia* 30 (1999), 301–15

Whitton, Kenneth, *The Theatre of Friedrich Dürrenmatt*, London: Oswald Wolff, 1980

Williams, Stephen, and Friell, Gerard, *The Rome that Did Not Fall: The Survival of the East in the Fifth Century*, London: Routledge, 1999

Wolfram, Herwig, *History of the Goths*, London: University of California Press, 1988

Wood, Ian, 'The End of Roman Britain: Continental Evidence and Parallels', in Michael Lapidge and David Dumville, *Gildas: New Approaches*, Woodbridge: Boydell Press, 1984

——, 'The Fall of the Western Empire and the End of Roman Britain', *Britannia* 18 (1987), 251–62

Index

185

Index

Frigeridus, Renatus 37
Fulgentius, St 115, 124–5
Fuqua, Antoine 9, 156

Geiseric, King 41
Gelasius, Pope 94, 112
Genoa 126
Gibbon, Edward 6, 11, 158
Gildas, St 14, 16, 39, 40–1
Giuliani, Rudolph 117
Gladwell, Malcolm 10
Glycerius, Emperor 64, 65, 96, 99, 125
Goldsborough 39–40
Gramsci, Antonio 145
Gratian, Emperor 25
Graves, Robert 148
Gregory the Great, Pope 31, 96
Gundobad 63–5

Hadrian, Emperor 86
Hadrian's Wall 38–9
Hannibal 27
Harries, Jill 15, 67
Heather, Peter 12, 29, 37, 52, 89
Henning, Dirk 77
Herculanus, possible brother of Romulus
    Augustulus 61
Hildebrandslied 133–9, 140
Hirohito, Emperor 87
Hitler, Adolf 116, 135, 149
Honorius 15, 23, 32, 33, 36–8, 40, 42,
    70–1, 75, 149
  rescript to Britain 39
Housesteads 38
Huns 43–5
  archaeology 44
  origins 28
Huntcliffe 39–40
Hydatius, Bishop 13–14, 15

Iatrus 31
Ildico 55
Illus 101–2
Illyria 35
Ischia 81

Isidore of Miletus 3
Isonzo river 105

James, Harold 158
Jerome, St 17, 23, 24, 25, 28, 35, 96
John I, Pope 124, 126, 128
John of Antioch 107
Johnson, Boris 157
Jordanes 54, 82, 85
  Getica 19
  Romana 19
Joviacum 93
Jozsef, Attila 139
Julian II, Emperor, the Apostate 2, 27, 62,
    77, 95, 122, 150
Julius II, pope 144
Julius Caesar 70, 150
Julius Nepos 9, 65–7, 74, 96, 100–1,
    125
  assassination 101
  diplomacy with Euric 68
  hoping for help from the East 5–6,
    72
  promotes Orestes 69–70
Justin, Emperor 125, 126, 128
Justin II, Emperor 132
Justinian, Emperor 2, 7, 9, 132

Karl I, Emperor 157
Kassel 133–5
King Arthur 9, 156
Kipling, Rudyard 139
Klimt, Gustav 135

Last Legion, The 9, 134, 154–6
Lavant-Kirchbichl 91–2
Lay of Hildebrand see Hildebrandslied
Leffler, Doug 9, 156
Legion 1, 'Italian' 31
Leo I, Emperor 63, 65, 66, 110–11
Leo I, pope, the Great 55, 61, 147
Leo II, Emperor 65, 73
Leo X, pope 144
Libanius 27
Liberius, Petrus Marcellinus Felix 121–4

Index